Dr David Fontana is the author of over 40 books on psychology, meditation, dreams, spirituality and psychical research that have been translated into 26 languages. His publications include *The Secret Language of Symbols*, *The Secret Language of Dreams*, *The Meditator's Handbook*, *Learn to Meditate*, *Psychology, Religion and Spirituality*, and most recently *Is There an Afterlife?* He is a PhD in psychology, a Fellow of the British Psychological Society, and a Past President of the Society of Psychical Research. Formerly Distinguished Visiting Fellow at Cardiff University, he is the first Professor of Transpersonal Psychology to be appointed in the UK. David Fontana has studied and practised meditation for over 30 years, working with leading teachers from many countries and traditions, and has been a frequent broadcaster on radio and television.

A Selection of Books by David Fontana

The Secret Language of Symbols
The Secret Language of Dreams
Meditating with Mandalas
The Elements of Meditation
The Lotus in the City
Know Who You Are, Be What You Want
Growing Together: Parent-Child Relationships as a Path to
*   Wholeness and Happiness*
Your Growing Child
Learn to Meditate
Learn Zen Meditation
The Meditator's Handbook
Meditation Week by Week
Psychology, Religion and Spirituality
Is There an Afterlife?

CREATIVE MEDITATION & VISUALIZATION

DAVID FONTANA

WATKINS PUBLISHING
LONDON

Distributed in the USA and Canada by Sterling Publishing Co., Inc.
387 Park Avenue South, New York, NY 10016

This edition first published in the UK and USA 2007 by
Watkins Publishing, Sixth Floor, Castle House,
75–76 Wells Street, London W1T 3QH

Designed and typeset by Jerry Goldie

ISBN13: 978-1-905857-30-2

Printed in the U.S.A

Contents

Introduction

This book describes and explains how to use one of the most important powers of the human mind, visualization. The mind is a wonderful instrument, surely among the most wonderful in creation, and it is a sad fact that very few of us make use of even a small part of its potential. We often hear (and probably use) the phrase 'mind over matter', yet to what extent do we really believe that mind can influence matter, that the mind – by taking thought – can affect the body and the things it is able to do?

Why is it that we neglect the power of the mind to such an extent? There are two main reasons. Firstly we are never taught how to use this power. The Western educational system is a wonderful tool for conveying information to children and young adults, but at no point does it devote any part of the curriculum to the way in which our own minds can bring benefits to our own bodies. Secondly, Western science has typically either taken little interest in the mind-body relationship, or has actively dismissed its importance. For example, it is only very recently that the medical profession has begun to accept that at least a third (and maybe significantly more) of physical illnesses have their origins at least partly in the mind. The same profession has just started to recognize the power of the mind to heal the body, even though what is now called the *placebo* effect – the fact that if you believe something is doing you good then there is fair chance that it will – has been demonstrated by the medical profession's own experiments for very many years. And it is even more recently that the same profession, together with the psychology profession, has begun to recognize that *visualization* is one of the most effective ways in which this mental power can be harnessed to best effect.

Visualization is in fact an important tool not only for assisting healing but for enhancing human performance in a wide range of areas, from sport to creativity and from social success to career advancement. This book looks at these areas and also links visualization to another power of the mind, neglected until recently by Western science, namely meditation. Visualization and meditation are not the same thing but they are closely related and can be used in harmony and conjunction with each other, particularly as visualization becomes even more effective if it is practised as a form of meditation. Meditation is about calming and quietening the mind, so that instead of being continually distracted by the chatter of its own thinking (much of it, we have to admit, of very little consequence) it becomes clear and open, a state in which it is much more effective in relaxing the body, in dealing with stress, and ultimately in gaining insights into its own deeper nature. Meditation practices differ in detail, but all are based upon giving the mind a stimulus – such as the breathing – on which it focuses steadily and to which it returns each time thoughts intrude and threaten to cause distractions. When combining meditation with visualization, the meditator uses visualized images as the stimulus, whether these have to do with healing, with remaining calm in stressful situations, or with any one of the many other activities with which visualization is helpful. Meditation also helps develop powers of concentration, so that the mind becomes more effective in holding onto visualized images more clearly and consistently whenever they prove helpful in daily life. And the better the concentration, the more likely it is that these images will bring results.

Naturally enough, visualization and meditation are not panaceas for all the challenges – some unwelcome, others welcome and freely chosen – with which life presents us (no such panaceas exist in this world) but visualization and meditation add a new and very effective dimension to life at both psychological and physical levels, and do so, moreover, at no cost apart from the expenditure of a little time and commitment. Results are, of course, not necessarily apparent overnight. Both visualization and meditation are natural activities of the mind but the great majority of us have allowed them to fall into disuse. In most cases we employed them better as children than we do now. We have to relearn our own skills, and like any learning this can take a little time. But it is not only time well spent, it is time that brings new and exciting discoveries about our own minds and about ourselves. The human mind is one of the most wonderful instruments in creation and one of the most interesting and most magical. Our mind is essentially where we live, and the link between our spiritual and our physical selves. Each of us must decide for him or herself why the mind should possess such riches when we normally only use – and indeed only discover – a small percentage of them, with the result that we go through much of life as partial strangers to ourselves. Visualization and meditation can take us deeper into these riches, and give us practical tools for enhancing life and making us more effective at all levels of our being.

Chapter 1

What is Visualization and Why does it Work?

Visualization and Imagination

The word *visualization* (sometimes referred to as *imagery*) suggests that we are talking about imaginary scenes that we picture in the mind's eye – and so we are, but there is much more to it than this. When asked to visualize, many people are indeed able to 'see' things in the mind's eye when they close their eyes, but others simply become aware of impressions and of thoughts that have to do with pictures rather than seeing the pictures themselves. Yet others report that they can 'see' visualizations even when their eyes are open, as if these visualizations are viewed by the so-called 'third eye' (said to be situated just above and between the physical eyes) and exist simultaneously with what is seen at the same time with normal vision. Each of these experiences can nevertheless be classed as visualization, and it is useful to try visualizing now for a moment to see which of them is true for you. Since this is your natural method of visualizing it is good to use it in all your visualization practice, at least until you have fully mastered the technique.

In addition, whether linguistically accurate or not, we can

further extend the term visualization so that it embraces other imaginary experiences that are not strictly visual but that are associated with the pictures we 'see'. For example we may conjure up a picture of the seashore and the waves breaking on the beach, and then spontaneously or deliberately add imaginary sounds to the picture so that we hear the waves, and even perhaps the sound of the wind and the cries of the seabirds. We can add imaginary tactile sensations, and feel the wind on our faces and the soft sand under our feet. We can go further still and include *feelings* as part of visual experiences. For example we may be using visualization to help us get back to fitness after an injury or an illness, and imagine ourselves running freely along the visualized seashore, and then accompany this with the *feeling* that we have all our usual energy and our usual pain-free mobility.

All these aspects of imagination can be included under the heading of visualization because they support and strengthen each other, making the whole imaginary experience not only more vivid but more likely to bring desired results. In other words, instead of thinking of *visual imagination, auditory imagination, tactile imagination* etc. as separate abilities, we can for present purposes combine them together, just as in real life our senses combine them to give us a unified experience. This does not mean we must necessarily put all these forms of imagination together every time we attempt to visualize. It is sufficient to remember that we can use more than one of them at a time if we wish to do so and if the exercise comes easily to us. Eventually, as our powers of visualization develop, so we will find that they tend to arise together spontaneously. As soon as we close our eyes and picture the seashore we hear the wind and the waves and feel the spray on our faces, the sand under our feet, and the exhilaration of moving with perfect health and abundant energy.

Developing Powers of Visualization

I mentioned the word *develop* in the last paragraph, and development forms one of the themes of the book. We can, with practice, quite rapidly develop our powers of visualization provided we have the will to do so and the interest and the commitment that go with it. Throughout the book there are boxes and references in the text to the exercises that help this development, and you will probably soon be able to add ideas of your own to these. Some you may find more helpful than others, but it is important to give them all a fair trial, after which you can concentrate more on the ones that appeal to you most.

The book is divided into chapters that cover, in turn, all the various ways in which visualization can be used to help your psychological, physical and spiritual development, and it is important to read them all. You may think, for example, that the chapter dealing with the use of visualization in sport is of little practical value to you as you do not take part in sport. Or you may think that the section in Chapter 2 on anxiety in examinations and public speaking is not relevant to you as you are not involved in either of these things. However, all the chapters are there not only to be of practical use to those who wish to use the information in daily life, but to give a comprehensive picture of what visualization can do, and its extraordinary – and I am happy to use the words mysterious and even mystical, for reasons that will, I hope, become clear as we go through the book – power to bring about changes in both our inner and our outer lives.

When you have been through the book and are satisfied you have a good picture of the nature, purpose and practice of visualization, you can use the chapters that have most practical relevance to you for reference purposes, but it is also valuable to keep a notebook of your own to record accounts of your practice and experiences, and to note down advice and suggestions to yourself. Keeping this kind of notebook is an invaluable aid to progress.

Box 1: Visualize Something Familiar

One way to familiarize yourself with the practice of visualization is to focus on common objects that you see nearly every day of your life. Let's use the main door into your house or apartment. As you will be doing the exercise with your eyes closed, read through it first and commit it to memory, or ask someone else to read it to you. Try to answer the questions in the order in which they are given.

If you are already a meditator, sit as you do in meditation. If work of this kind is new to you sit in a chair or crossed-legged on the floor, whichever feels more comfortable. Close your eyes and focus for a minute or two on your breathing in order to help relax the mind.

Switch your attention to a point either behind your closed eyes or in the centre of the forehead just above them. Now imagine you are looking at the main door of your house. What colour is it? Does it have a window and a letterbox? If so, how do they look? Can you see the keyhole? What is the door made of and what condition is it in? What feelings does it arouse in you – pride, a sense of welcome, disappointment at its appearance? If you open the door what is the first thing you see?

Now open your eyes and think about the exercise. How were you able to get the information to answer the questions? Did you 'see' the door or just have thoughts about it? Did you notice that by making you look closer at the door, the questions helped you to see it more clearly? Did you find that visualizing the door engaged your feelings about it? When you opened the door did you 'see' more clearly still?

It is always useful to make a list of the things you have learnt.

Visualization and the Psycho-Spiritual and Mystery Traditions

The terms *psycho-spiritual traditions* and *mystery traditions* are used frequently throughout the book, as it is these traditions that have, over many centuries, done most to develop the visualization practices that are now becoming recognized by Western science as enhancing human health, happiness and performance in a wide range of areas. The term *psycho-spiritual traditions* refers to the world's great spiritual traditions such as Hinduism, Buddhism, Taoism, Judaism, Christianity and Islam, all of which are not only religions but profound psychologies characterized by a deep understanding of the mind and of human behaviour, and of the practices that bring about personal and spiritual growth. Modern Western scientific psychology is little more than 100 years old, and although it has made great progress in helping us deal with psychological problems, it has not in any way supplanted the insights provided by the great traditions. A small number of particularly enlightened psychologists, such as Carl Jung, have drawn deeply upon these traditions in their own work, but it is only in recent years that more (although still regrettably few) Western psychologists have begun taking an interest in them and in the spiritual aspects of man (the area of psychology concerned is now referred to as *transpersonal psychology*, since it studies the levels 'trans' – i.e. beyond – the limited personal self).

Western religions, as well as Eastern religions, are included in the list of traditions given above, as visualization and other meditation practices have always been part of their tradition, although much less public emphasis is given to them. In Christianity they have, for the most part, been exclusive to initiates such as priests and monks, partly because the Church claimed for itself the role of intermediary between man and God. This is unfortunate, and is one reason why so many people in the West, seeking spiritual practices, have looked to Eastern religions rather than to Christianity. Only now are these practices becoming better known and taught by the Christian Church.

The term *mystery traditions* refers to the hidden traditions that have always been part of deeper levels of Western thought. Sometimes referred to as 'occult' – a term that simply means 'hidden' but has often been taken to refer to so-called black magic and other nefarious practices – the mystery traditions represent the esoteric side of Western spirituality, that is the side that tradition- ally was only taught to initiates, as opposed to the exoteric side that was available to all believers. Having their origins in Ancient Greece and Egypt, and perhaps brought to the West even earlier than this from India, the mystery traditions were kept secret because it was felt that they would become distorted and debased by people who had not had the necessary training to put them into practice or who came to them with selfish and misguided motives. In addition, these traditions suffered persecution from the Christian Churches, which recognized their power and feared that their teachings, which held that men and women could be helped to find their own path to the Divine, would weaken the authority of the priesthood. As a consequence, many of the practices central to the mystery traditions have never become generally known. Initiates, who were sworn to secrecy, kept their oath, and the traditions virtually died out, overtaken by the increasing commercialism and materialism that took hold of all the great civilizations.

What are the Benefits of Visualization and Why does it Work?

Visualization is an extraordinary tool for obtaining results in so many areas of life. Put simply, we can say that visualization is the art of helping us obtain desired goals by picturing ourselves actually achieving them. I am not talking about winning the lottery or getting a new car or obtaining a rise at work. There are people who claim that visualization can be used for such things, but this book is not about making your fortune. It aims rather higher than that. Its purpose is to explain how visualization can be used as an aid to healing and to good physical health, to dealing with common psychological problems, to improving sporting abilities and to furthering self-exploration, self-understanding and spiritual development. If you wish to use the information it contains for other purposes then this is up to you, and you can experiment as you please, but I must warn you that the spiritual and mystical traditions that have practised visualization success-fully for centuries insist that it should only be used for positive helpful purposes. They tell us that those who try to use it to harm others invariably find that the harm rebounds upon themselves. Visualization should never be used for selfish or harmful purposes.

How does visualization work? To answer this question we must say a little about the conscious and the unconscious levels of the mind. Not surprisingly, we assume that the conscious level, the level at which we think, hope, plan and make decisions is by far the most important. After all, we 'live' mostly in our conscious mind. It is our conscious mind that tells us who we are and how we are feeling, and it is through our conscious mind that we relate to the world. However, below the level of consciousness lies the vast reservoir of the unconscious. It is from the unconscious that our thoughts actually arise, and it is the unconscious that stores our memories – not only those we can access whenever we wish but the much larger collection that we assume we have forgotten but that in reality continue to play a major part in our psychology. Although we are usually unaware of it, the unconscious memory influences our emotional lives, our attitudes, important aspects of our personalities, our likes and dislikes, and even causes our irrational and deep-seated fears and anxieties and many of the things about ourselves that we do not properly understand. These unconscious memories often emerge in dreams or in response to events, as when a popular song from years ago reminds us of our first love, or the sight of the sea reminds us of childhood holidays. Memories forgotten for many years can sometimes also be accessed by hypnosis, or by psychotherapeutic techniques such as Freudian or Jungian psychoanalysis. It has even been claimed that we may never completely forget anything that happens to us, and that all our life memories are stored away at various levels of the unconscious.

Among other authorities, the great Swiss psychiatrist and psychotherapist, Carl Jung, considered that the unconscious mind is not only in touch with our personal life-history (the *personal unconscious*) but at a deeper level with what he called the *collective unconscious*, a kind of psychological blueprint that, as Jung (1968) puts it, 'is not a personal acquisition but is inborn ...' and that leads to 'modes of behaviour that are more or less the same everywhere and in all individuals. It is, in other words, identical in all men and thus constitutes a common psychic substrate ... which is present in every one of us.' The collective unconscious thus predisposes us to respond in broadly similar ways to many of life's experiences, and ensures that human beings remain identifiably similar as a species in their psychological makeup. But in Jung's view it does even more than this since it contains the *archetypes* – concepts that have been with humankind since earliest times and that emerge into consciousness in all cultures and across the centuries in the form of universally recognizable ideas and ideals such as the 'hero', the 'divine child', 'the wise old man', 'the Earth mother', the 'Holy Trinity', the 'Holy Grail' and many of the other themes that occur in the great spiritual traditions of East and West. Archetypal images also arise in symbolic form in our dreams and in all the great myths and legends of the world, and our ability to recognize their meaning and the part they play in our inner lives is an important factor in our psychological and spiritual development. We also unconsciously project the archetypes outwards, using them to make sense of some of the mysteries of existence. They are the source of many of our higher longings, and are one of the forces that prompt us to seek answers to deeper questions such as the meaning of life, the true nature of the self and of the soul, the path to the Creator, and the existence of other dimensions of reality. Archetypal energies are also one of the main sources of our more sublime creative urges and abilities, and when denied and repressed are one of the principal causes of that existential dissatisfaction with life that has long been a feature of Western civilization.

The deeper we go into both the personal and the collective levels of the unconscious, the more we find that the 'language' with which it communicates to us consists of images and pictures rather than words. The collective unconscious and parts of the personal unconscious are in fact associated with those parts of the brain/mind that developed in the early stages of humankind's evolutionary journey, long before the ability to use words emerged. Our relationship with the unconscious does in fact depend largely upon our ability to use images and pictures, and it may be that images and pictures are the only effective way in which communication with the collective unconscious becomes possible. This explains why visualization exercises are such an effective way for exploring the unconscious and for utilizing its powers to help us progress in the important areas of life described in this book.

Why is communication with the unconscious such a valuable aid towards this progress? The mind is not a blank slate at birth, as was once supposed. It is programmed to allow us to do many things, from sucking at the breast and walking, to acquiring language, mathematical and other skills. All our deeper qualities, from love and empathy to delight in the beauties of nature and the arts, are already there, and deeper still, linked to the collective unconscious there are levels of wisdom and understanding of whose existence we may not even dream unless we deliberately set out to seek them. Gurdjieff, the Russian mystic and teacher, truly said that we each live in a beautiful mansion, yet all too often fail to move out of the basement. Much of this book is about a way out of the basement, and the visualization and other meditative methods that help us find it.

However, not only does the unconscious have a profound influence upon us, we can also have a profound influence upon it, and much of this book is also about how we can use this influence and how the results can enrich and enhance our lives. Simply by visualizing what we wish to achieve, whether it be physical healing or levels of performance in chosen fields or desired psychological and spiritual qualities, it is possible to convey to the unconscious the message that this is not only something for which we are striving, but that this is something that is actually within reach. The mental picture, for example, of ourselves acting kindly or confidently in a situation that usually produces the opposite effect in us, can not only inspire the confidence that such a thing is indeed possible, but help produce the inner psychological changes that make it happen. By enlisting the help of the unconscious in this way, some of the emphasis is taken off the conscious mind, which previously supposed it was the only agency that could attempt to bring about these changes (in reality, the conscious mind can frequently get in the way of progress towards the desired goal by trying too hard).

Visualization practices can be so effective in enlisting the help of the unconscious that many people have argued that visualization is in fact a magical act, and certainly it has featured prominently in the practices of the various magical traditions across the centuries, all of which have in common the notion that, by producing changes in the inner world of the mind, changes can be brought about in the outer world of physical reality. Alchemy, for example, which has long been derided as a naïve attempt to turn base metal into gold through the use of a magical substance known as the philosopher's stone (not a piece of rock but a powder) was in reality a sophisticated process of inner change that transformed the base metal of the self into the gold of spiritual enlightenment. Only when this change was successful was it believed that equivalent changes and benefits could be produced in the outer world (it was the Swiss psychiatrist and psychologist

Carl Jung who drew proper attention to the real purpose of alchemy (Jung 1956).

Humans Have Always Visualized

Visualizing involves creating a mental image, either of things as they are or of things as you hope they might be. It is not known whether animals visualize or not, but humans have been doing it from prehistoric times. Man is often said to have begun his ascent from primitive to modern with the development of tool-making and of speech during the Pleistocene or Great Ice Age period (1.64 million to 10,000 years ago), but this ignores the fact that the ability to visualize must also have played a major part. Humans started to visualize some time during the Pleistocene period, as witnessed by their ability to create figurative art. One cannot make a drawing of a wild animal on the inner walls of a cave, illuminated only by the flickering light of a fire, unless one has a mental picture of what the animal looks like. The cave paintings at Lascaux and at Pech-Merle in France and at Tassili-des-Ajjer in North Africa and elsewhere reveal great skill in visualization – in fact, both of the forms of visualization mentioned above, namely visualization of things as they are and of things as the artist would have them be. On the one hand, animals are shown running freely, and on the other, as prey for the hunter. The implication is that by visualizing and representing animals as prey, the artist believed that their death at the hands of the persuing hunters would magically be assured.

The representation of things as one wishes them to be demonstrates the important role that imagination plays in visualization. In fact, imagination and visualization are inextricably linked. For example, when some 50,000 years ago humans developed a belief in (or received evidence for) life after death and buried the dead with provisions and weapons to help them on their journey to the next world, cave paintings began to depict human figures participating in what appear to be religious or magical ceremonies designed to ensure a safe passage of the dead to the next world or possibly even to illustrate what takes place on arrival there. The idea that the person lives on in a different form even when you are confronted with their lifeless body is a highly sophisticated one. Psychic abilities might have allowed some individuals to see or hear the departed, just as even in our materialistic age approximately 40 per cent of bereaved wives and husbands report some sensory contact with a partner after his or her death (see Fontana 2005). But along with the belief that the inner life survived the death of the physical body there must have been a direct awareness of the value of this inner life, and imagination, visualization and associated experiences, such as visions and dreams, must have played a part in the growth of this awareness.

If we now come forward in history to around 8000–7000 BCE, we find that the nomadic, hunter-gatherer lifestyle that had endured for the previous 100,000 years changed relatively abruptly into that of settled urban living, made possible by the development of agriculture. By 4000 BCE many of the communities in Mesopotamia (modern Iraq) were practising irrigation and developing extensive trading connections, and the arts and crafts that accompanied these advances are regarded as marking the start of recorded history. The Sumerians who inhabited the extensive central plain enjoyed a period of great prosperity and built elaborate shrines and great temples that housed beautifully worked figurines in silver, copper and stone, and wall paintings of exceptional quality. Excavations at the site of the city of Uruk have uncovered the first examples of attempts at written language and, significantly, these take the form of *pictures*, representing familiar objects such as boats, sheep, pigs, oxen, ploughs and many other items indispensable for trade and agriculture.

Taken together, the above facts all bear witness to a remarkable ability to visualize. It is impossible to build temples – some estimated to be as large as the Gothic masterpieces of northern

Europe created thousands of years later – or to make exquisite representations of animal and human forms and to develop and use a written pictorial language unless one has the ability to form and hold images in the mind. In Ur, one of the great cities of Sumeria, vast tombs have been unearthed furnished with massive quantities of gold and silver and finely wrought jewellery that provide testimony of the continuing belief in an afterlife. There is also abundant evidence throughout the period of a belief in a supreme god (Enlil) and of subordinate deities such as Ningal, the moon goddess. There is equally extensive evidence of schools for the young that taught language and stories about the gods and heroes such as Gilgamesh, together with details of the underworld to which souls journeyed after death and even of the Great Flood and of one man's escape from it in an ark. Babylon in northern Sumeria, another seat of learning and culture, has also provided us with outstandingly beautiful artefacts and detailed historical information. The art produced in Sumeria during these centuries is in fact among the most breathtaking and impressive in recorded history, and its power is ample testimony to the visionary genius of those responsible for its creation.

In the centuries after the decline of the great cities of Sumeria, arts and crafts of comparable quality were produced by the Hittites (in what is now modern Turkey) and the Assyrians (modern Syria) and elsewhere in the Middle East, but it is the outpouring of artistic excellence in Lower and Upper Egypt that most captures our imagination. From the first dynasty (approximately 3100 BCE) onwards, Egyptian civilization achieved a level of cultural distinction that is one of the finest examples of man's creative genius. There is no space to do justice to this remarkable period in human history, but two examples that throw particular light on the power of visualization are firstly, the Egyptian representation of the gods and secondly, their concepts of an afterlife.

The Use of Symbols

The major Egyptian gods are typically depicted as having the heads of animals: Thoth the god of wisdom, has the head of an ibis bird; Ammut, the underworld goddess – the head of a crocodile; Horus, the god of the sky – the head of a falcon; Anubis, the god of cemeteries – the head of a jackal; Bastet, the moon goddess – the head of a cat; Nut, the sky goddess – the head of a cow (Hathor, the mother of Horus, is also shown with the head of a cow); Khnum, the god who shaped humans on his potter's wheel – the head of a ram; Seth, the god of chaos and violence – the head of an imaginary composite scorpionlike creature, and so on (see Hart 1986). In spite of this use of animal figures, it is highly unlikely the Egyptians thought of the gods as animals. Animals were a visionary concept, at a time when written language was unavailable to all but the priesthood, of symbolizing the qualities that the gods represented. Horus, the all-seeing lord of the skies, was symbolized by the falcon because the falcon is the most commanding and far-seeing of birds; Anubis, who conducted the souls of the departed to the next world, was symbolized by the jackal because the jackal was known to frequent cemeteries and places of the dead; Bastet, the moon goddess, was symbolized by the cat because the cat is a nocturnal animal who shares something of her mystery; Thoth, the god of wisdom, was symbolized by the ibis because the ibis appears grave and wise; and Seth was symbolized by an imaginary creature as his dark powers were beyond anything that could be represented by a known animal.

For these symbols of the gods to have been effective in ancient Egypt (and the number of surviving images of their animal heads tells us that they were effective for centuries) individuals must have been able to hold visual images of them in the mind. Imagine how ineffective the word 'falcon' would be as a symbol of the sky-god Horus if you were unable to conjure up an image of what a falcon looks like. For the symbol to work, one must have the picture of a falcon firmly in the mind, its keen eyes, its powerful beak, its ability to soar high in the sky and to see the world below literally for miles around. Similarly, how effective would the symbol of a cat be for the moon goddess, Bastet, if you were unable to remember what a cat actually looks like? For the ancient Egyptians – and equally for us today – the basic ability to visualize could be developed until the mental images of the gods became as clear and as sharp to us as if they were being seen in reality. Some might argue that this personalized the archetypal energies that the gods represented into semi-human forms that were not what these energies actually were, but this argument misunderstands the nature of symbols. As Carl Jung emphasized, archetypal energies are abstractions that only become known to us when they emerge into consciousness in symbolic form. One does not mistake the symbol for the reality that it represents, but at the same time the symbol is a way of helping us encounter this reality. As we shall stress at other points in this book, symbols (as opposed to what Freud and Jung both referred to as *signs*, which are devices such as logos and trademarks simply thought up by the conscious mind) are things that arise spontaneously from the collective consciousness as reflections of the archetypes, and thus are found to have a universal meaning across cultures and across the centuries. They epitomize something of the *qualities* of the archetypes, thus allowing us to arrive at an understanding, however limited, of their nature, and to draw closer to experiencing their power.

If the Egyptians wished to relate, for example, to Horus, and to realize within themselves something of his perceptive and far-sighted abilities, then one way of doing so was to focus upon his falcon-headed image in meditation, with the mind clear of distractions, and at the end of the meditation to visualize him soaring into the sky to symbolize the freedom of the spirit from the constraints of the physical world. Visualization meditations such as this remain part of the practices used by the great spiritual traditions of the Eastern world, in particular Hinduism and Buddhism. Variants are now used effectively in many of the psychotherapeutic practices of modern psychology, particularly in *transpersonal psychology*, the area of the subject that studies spiritual experiences, altered states of consciousness, practices such as meditation and visualization, creative experiences and all those episodes in life, real or imaginary, that appear to take us beyond (i.e. *trans*) the limited physical self.

Geometrical Symbols

Symbols and their meaning and use in visualization are discussed more fully in Chapter 6, but in view of their importance it is appropriate to try a visualization exercise (Box 2) using symbols. The easiest symbols to use are geometrical ones. Geometrical symbols are part of the innate language of the unconscious, and have been with humankind for centuries. We find that they carry much the same meaning right across cultures. For example, the circle symbolizes the idea of wholeness, of completion and, because it has no beginning and no end, eternity and the Divine. The square symbolizes solidity, dependability, and, by virtue of its four corners, the four directions, and the four elements. The cross symbolizes the descent of the spirit (the downward stroke) into the material world (the horizontal stroke). The triangle, depending upon which way it is pointing, symbolizes the upward movement of the human spirit towards the heavens and the downward movement of creative energy towards the earth (when these two movements are combined, symbolized by putting the two triangles together, we get the six-pointed star).

The Hindu traditions link these symbols even more closely to the elements through the so-called *tattvas* system. In this system a yellow square is taken to represent earth, a silver crescent on its back to represent water, a blue circle to represent air, a red triangle to represent fire, and a black oval to represent the spirit. The specific use of these symbols for visualization meditation will be explained in Chapter 7, but they obviously gain in symbolic power through their combination of shape, colour, and the four visible elements (earth, air, fire and water) and one invisible element (ether or spirit) that go to make up the physical world and our own bodies. Box 2 presents the visualization exercise.

The Ancient Greeks

The ancient Greeks regarded the world as designed on the basis of geometry, which to them had a mystical power. Pythagorus, the great Greek geometrician, astronomer and mathematician, taught geometry as one of the subjects in the mystery school (an academy in which students were initiated into the deeper mysteries of life and death), which he founded in the sixth century BCE. We know little of their practices, which must certainly have involved visualization but which were kept secret even at the time, although we do know that the Greeks as a culture put visualization to good practical use. As with the early civilizations already mentioned, we know this from a study of their artistic artefacts, particularly sculptures. Greek sculpture is probably – I should say certainly – the finest the Western world has ever produced, even though it takes us back over 2,000 years in time. See examples in the National Museum in Athens if you can, but if not, try at least to study pictures. When you look at the pictures try to visualize the sculptures as if you can see them from all sides. Imagine touching them, feeling the cool shape of the marble, the extraordinarily satisfying tactile contact. Visualize them not as inert stone but as living representatives of a divine vision. For the Greek sculptor, the perfect form – the symbol of the god or goddess or hero (a man with the potential to be raised up to the divine pantheon, as was Hercules) in human form – was already present within the virgin marble. His task was to manifest from within himself the art that would enable this form to be revealed. For him, the stone was ready to disclose the divine image, provided he could become one with the stone and allow himself to be the instrument for this magical transformation.

Box 2: Using Geometrical Symbols

Symbols are mentioned frequently in this book, and have played a major part in the visualization practices of all the mystery and occult traditions. One major advantage is that many of them are particularly easy to visualize. This is especially true of symbols such as the circle, the cross, and the triangle.

Select one of these symbols and if possible draw it accurately on a sheet of paper. Use a *tattva* colour (yellow for the square, silver crescent on a dark background for water, blue for the circle and red for the triangle) and put the result on a wall or a shelf.

Sit comfortably, as for meditation, and focus upon your breathing for a minute or two, with your eyes open. Now look steadily at the symbol in front of you (or close your eyes and imagine it if you don't have a picture of it). Try to fix it in your mind. When you think you have done so, close your eyes, as if you are taking a photograph of it, and hold the image in your visual memory for as long as you can.

When the image fades, open your eyes, and carry out the exercise again. Repeat it if necessary so that you have done it for a total of five times, but no more (the exercise can become rather mechanical if repeated too often). From time to time during the day close your eyes and try to 'see' the symbol again. Carry out the exercise at least once a day until you are satisfied you can visualize the image clearly.

When you are satisfied you can do this, as a follow-up try changing the colours of the image. Use all the *tattva* colours in turn. Finish by reverting to the original colour. Now try the same exercise using the other *tattva* images. Carry out this exercise at least once a day until you are satisfied you can visualize all the images clearly and change their colours. Always conclude by visualizing each image in its original colour.

Approximately how long were you able to keep the image in your mind each time? Sometimes it fades, and sometimes it slides away to one side. Either way, notice how short the visualization span is before we start training it.

In order to imagine satisfactorily that things exist, we need to be able to visualize them, to make our thoughts concrete within the magic theatre of the mind. Look, for example, at story books for very young children. If the wind is one of the characters in the story, then it is shown as a face puffing out its cheeks and blowing all before it. If the sun is represented it takes the form of a smiling face. Even objects that already have a concrete existence are transformed so that the child can relate more intimately to them. Trees and even houses are all given faces, while animals who already have faces are humanized not only by wearing clothes but by adopting human expressions such as smiles and frowns.

To the ancients Greeks visualizations, like dreams, were thought to come sometimes from the gods, and in spite of the advances of modern science we still do not know the origin of these mental pictures. We know which parts of the brain are involved, but how can the physical electrochemical energy of the brain produce non-physical events like visualizations and thoughts? I shall have more to say about this mystery at various points in the book, but the Ancients may have been correct in supposing that a non-material reality works *through* the physical matter of the body rather than originating from it.

Across the centuries we find that visualization has played a vital role in Western culture. Once again some of the best evidence comes from works of art and architecture. For example, in the 13th century there was a sudden flowering of cathedral building, in particular the great Gothic cathedrals of France, the UK and elsewhere in western Europe. There was no direct precedent for these magnificent, awe-inspiring works of architecture, art and engineering. Suddenly, as if their builders were inspired by some direct revelation, they began to appear in all their beauty and complexity. We know little about the architects, the master masons and the stone carvers who created them, but it is unlikely they grew piecemeal from a few sketchy ideas and depended upon trial and error mixed with massive doses of good fortune for their success. They could only have been the flowering of a series of extraordinary visions that appear to have occurred all over northern Europe during that brief period of the 13th century. From the soaring Gothic pillars and ceilings that mirrored in stone the overarching branches of great forests to the lacelike fragility of some of the carvings they represent a paean of praise to the Almighty that had and still has the ability to alter the consciousness of all who experience them with sufficiently receptive minds.

If we come forward again in time to the Renaissance, born in Italy in the 15th and 16th centuries, and look at the art and craft that marked it out as one of the most creatively inspired periods in European history, we are faced as before with artefacts that challenge and inspire us to such an extent that they change our concepts of what it means to be human. The paintings of Leonardo da Vinci, Michelangelo, Raphael, Caravaggio and Titian and the sculptures of Michelangelo, Donatello and many others represent a rebirth of the visions of the ancient Greeks and speak to us as intimately and directly now as when they were first given life. Although many Renaissance artists worked from nature and from male and female models, their paintings are much more than reproductions of what was visible to the physical eye. Their inner visions transformed what they saw, giving their paintings a unique quality that allows experts, even centuries later, to identify them one from another (their work is rarely signed). Other Renaissance artists, such as Botticelli, Bernini and Poussin, appear to have been inspired primarily by their inner visions, as were later 19th-century artists such as Moreau, the members of the so-called Pre-Raphaelite Brotherhood particularly William Holman Hunt, John Everett Millais and Dante Gabriel Rossetti and later the French Impressionists such as Monet and Manet, Bernard and Cézanne. And what can we say of Picasso, one of the greatest artists of modern times, except that his inner visions revolutionized not only modern art but the way in which the 20th century saw the world. Does anyone seriously suppose that Picasso produced his extraordinary images by daubing away haphazardly just to see what effect he might produce by trial and error? I doubt it.

The Mystery and Occult Traditions

Great artists each have their own way of utilizing visualizations in their work. Salvador Dali, one of the great exponents of surrealism (a term meaning the superimposition of irrational dream images upon those of the waking world), made use of the visions that fleetingly cross the mind during the hypnogogic state, the state half-way between waking and sleeping when the mind is beginning to lose its hold on waking reality and to open itself to the images spawned in such profusion by the unconscious. Dali is reported as sitting dozing over a table, with his chin supported lightly by a table fork. Each time his doze passed from the hypnogogic state into genuine sleep his head would fall forward and the pressure of his chin on the fork would wake him, leaving him with memories of the surreal visions he had just been experiencing. And it was these visions, in which the dream and the waking landscape are inextricably mingled, that formed the subject matter of some of his most striking works of art.

However, in the West it is the mystery and occult traditions that have made the most systematic use of visualization. 'Mystery' and 'occult' both refer simply to the fact that these traditions were *hidden* or *secret*. Only those individuals who were accepted into membership of these traditions could expect to be initiated into their practices, the great majority of which were designed to develop awareness of spiritual dimensions of reality and to enable the initiate to contact and enter these dimensions, thus realizing the eternal nature of the soul and its relationship to the Divine. Less well known is the fact that such mystery or occult practices were not limited to these magical and hermetic fraternities. All the great religions have their esoteric (i.e. private) as well as their exoteric (public) traditions. The esoteric traditions are largely the preserve of the priesthood and of monastic communities, and those breakaway groups – such as the Gnostic movement within early Christianity – who have sought to make them more generally available have been branded as heretical and their members subjected to persecution by the formal traditions, on the grounds that such esoteric knowledge should be left to the ecclesiastical hierarchies and not made available to laypeople. The reason for such a narrow view was that if the mysteries are accessible to all those who seek them, then the authority of the priesthood, which sees itself as the only intermediary between the Divine and man, is threatened and may be lost. Times have changed of course, and medieval persecutions have disappeared from Europe, nevertheless there is still a distinction between esoteric and exoteric, the latter freely available and the former requiring to be sought by those who want deeper levels of understanding.

The mystery traditions have their known origin in the various cultures that grew up around the Mediterranean basin at the time of the ancient Greeks. The initiates in these traditions took an oath of secrecy (it is said that failure to keep the oath was punishable by death), and so faithfully was this observed that we have no very clear idea of their methods and practices. However, they seem to have involved, among other things, out-of-body experiences in which the initiate left – or had the impression of leaving – his body and of travelling to the next world. It is said that such experiences removed all fear of death and dying, and gave the initiate access to levels of wisdom impossible to achieve simply by rational thought. We know from later traditions, to which I return shortly, that these experiences probably involved intense visualization practices. Put simply, the initiate was first taught to imagine that his consciousness, usually located within the physical body, could be positioned at a specific point outside it. So vivid were the visualizations essential to these imaginative experiences that, with practice, the initiate felt as if his consciousness was indeed able to pass at will outside the confines of the body and to look back and see the physical body like a discarded garment. At this point, it was said that the consciousness was genuinely outside the body, and could bring back knowledge of the next world when it returned to the physical dimension (we return to this subject in Chapter 6).

The Hermetic Tradition

Knowledge of these practices, although kept secret from public gaze, persisted within the various secret fraternities that replaced the early mystery traditions despite being forbidden by hierarchical Christianity. These fraternities, said in most cases to be 'Hermetic' in that they claimed descent from the real or legendary Hermes Trismegistus ('Thrice Great Hermes') said to have been a great Egyptian magician taught by – or actually embodying – both Thoth, the Egyptian god of wisdom and mouthpiece of the gods, and Hermes, the Greek messenger of the gods responsible for bringing this wisdom to earth. Hermes Trismegistus is claimed to have written 42 books, containing all magical lore, which were then stored in the great library of Alexandria but only fragments of which survived the burning of the library circa CE 641 subsequent to the Arab conquest of Alexandria. These fragments, known as the 'Hermetica' and translated into many languages, include 'The Divine Pymander' and 'The Vision', and together record variously how divine wisdom was revealed to Hermes, how he spread this wisdom throughout the world, the nature of this wisdom, hints of the vast domains beyond the threshold between the visible and the invisible worlds, and the spiritual development of the soul. The 'Hermetica' serves as the major foundation of all the mystery and occult traditions of the West. The best known of the surviving fragments is the so-called 'Emerald Tablet' (or 'Table'), claimed to be inscribed with the whole of Egyptian philosophy including the magical secrets of creation, and said to have been originally found in his hand when the body of Hermes Trismegistus was discovered in a cave tomb. Translated into Latin at the beginning of the 13th century CE, the 'Emerald Tablet' contains the frequently quoted statement:

> *That which is above is like that which is below …*
> *And as all things have been derived from one …*
> *So all things are born from this one.*

Usually shortened to 'As Above so Below', this statement is taken to mean that the physical world (the microcosm) is a reflection, albeit a shadowy and imperfect one, of the higher worlds, and can only be fully understood in the light of knowledge of these higher worlds. The alchemists, who believed that the base metal of the human soul could be transformed by appropriate practices into the pure gold of the spirit, placed particular emphasis upon the teachings of the 'Emerald Tablet', and considered that its mystical secrets were presented in the form of allegories (one of the probable reasons for the deliberately obscure and allegorical nature of most alchemical texts).

Many of the teachings contained in the various books of the 'Hermetica' date back at least to the first century CE and probably long before. They appear to be a compendium of Platonic and neo-Platonic philosophy, Egyptian magical teachings, and Judaic and Kabbalistic mysticism. Some authorities consider they had an important influence upon early Christianity, and certain passages do bear resemblances to the Gospel of St John and to the 12 books of the Gnostic gospels (such as the Gospel of St Philip, the Treatise on Resurrection, the Apocalypse of Peter, and the Gospel of St Thomas) found at Naj Hammadi in Upper Egypt in 1945, where they had seemingly been hidden for safety after the conversion of the Roman Empire to Christianity in the 4th century CE and the ruthless persecution of Gnosticism denounced as heretical by Christian bishops for some 200 years. Probably dating from the first century CE, at least some of the Gnostic gospels appear close in time to the later biblical gospels, and it is possible that at least the Gospel of St Thomas, which consists entirely of sayings by Jesus, may derive from one of the gospel sources.

Some of the tenets of Gnosticism, such as the idea that this world was created by a lesser deity in defiance of God, and the strange notion that it constitutes in fact the hell realms, have virtually disappeared from modern Western esoteric thought. However tenets such as these were not part of the Hermetic tradition; its magical practices, focused particularly on visualization, were intended to transform the human soul and enable it to rise up towards God or the gods, and bore no resemblance to the mumbo jumbo of spells and curses with which magic has become associated in the popular mind or with the sleight of hand of conjurors that now masquerades under the title of magic.

When we think of the Hermetic tradition and the many magical and occult fraternities to which it gave rise, we think of aged scholars poring through small eyeglasses over enormous dusty tomes in cobwebbed studies and workshops adorned with strange Hermetic and Kabbalistic symbols and (in the case of alchemists) with mysterious glass flasks, retorts and other paraphernalia necessary in the search for the 'chemycal wedding' (or 'chemical wedding to give it modern spelling) that would transmute not only the base metal of mankind but all base metal into the primary substance from which all creation arose. The aged scholars are invariably male, since traditionally the Hermetic traditions have appealed more to men, while women have been drawn to nature magic (currently both sexes take an equal interest in the two traditions). The reference to scholarship is equally correct because the Hermetic tradition is a path of wisdom as well as a path of visualization and meditation. We shall have more to say about this in the next section where we look at the Jewish Kabbalistic tradition (borrowed by Christian occultists from the 13th century CE onwards). So profound and complex is this tradition that Jewish Kabbalists insist no one should be accepted as a student until he has reached the age of 40, and only then if he has already spent many years studying the rich and extensive opus of the rest of Hebrew scholarship, in particular the Torah, the first five books of the Old Testament.

The Kabbalah

Hebrew scholarship is also intimately associated with the Kabbalah, which is the very heart of Jewish mysticism and which is said to have been given by God to Adam, and then passed down to Noah and subsequently to Abraham and to Moses. Its power and profundity as a mystical system is such that it was adopted by esoteric Christianity which recognized its power, and from there, in various forms (usually referred to as *cabala*), it has come to serve as the basis for the visualization practices used by many of the mystery traditions to which we refer below. Many books have been written on the kabbalah, the study of which is said to be primarily a masculine preserve only to be undertaken over many years of committed study and practice, under the guidance of an advanced teacher who has himself trodden the mystical Kabbalistic path.

The Kabbalah is far too complex to be dealt with in any detail here (see Lancaster 2006 for an excellent introduction) but, very briefly, it teaches that God created the world through 32 paths of wisdom, namely the 10 *sephirot* (*sephira* singular, *sephirot* plural) and the 22 letters of the Hebrew alphabet. We can touch only upon the former paths, which are described as ten attributes of God and which together provide the structure of all that exists. The ten *sephirot* together form what is usually called the Tree of Life, and the tree is therefore a kind of map or diagram that illustrates both the descent of God into the material world and the means by which humankind can, in turn, ascend to God.

It is the issue of ascent that features most prominently in the Western mystery traditions. The student of these traditions, who is introduced to the *sephirot*, is taught to rise upwards through each of them (a sequence sometimes referred to as 'rising through the planes') using specific visualizations at each point in order to reach towards the Divine. We will return to the details of this ascent in Chapter 7, and simply say here that the seven lower *sephirot* – respectively and in ascending order – the Kingdom, the Foundation, Glory, Victory, Beauty, Power and Loving Kindness – are levels of attainment or knowledge, while the three higher *sephirot* – Understanding, Wisdom and the Crown – are mystical levels of consciousness leading finally to the Divine.

The Tarot

Various attempts have been made by Western mystery traditions to link the *sephirot* with the Tarot cards and we return to these in Chapter 7, but something must be said here about the Tarot, since it has been so closely linked with the Western mystery traditions and particularly with visualization practices. If you are not familiar already with the 22 cards of the Tarot known as the *major arcana* (the rest of the pack, known as the *minor arcana*, are of no concern to us here) you may wish to get to know the cards now. Some techniques for using the cards in visualization are given in Chapter 7 and the importance of the major arcana is that each card represents one of the fundamental archetypal energies with which we are born and that go to make up part of the collective unconscious. These energies give us the potential to develop mentally and emotionally as human beings. We each differ in the relative strength of these respective archetypal energies, nevertheless, the major arcana provides us with an early psychological textbook that lists them for us, albeit in pictures rather than in words. Having read this far you will know that pictures arise from an older part of the mind than words, and not only represent a universal language but provide us with symbolic keys that help us to find our way back into this undiscovered country that lies deep within ourselves.

The origin of the cards is lost in history, though there are many theories linking them with India or with ancient Egypt. They have stood the test of time, which indicates their universal appeal. Currently there are many different versions on the market, and the oldest of these is the Marseille Pack, which is, thus, the most authentic although it lacks colour and excitement compared with some of the modern packs. It is very much a matter of choosing which pack appeals to you most. They almost all adhere to the 22 cards of the Marseille Pack, although the main symbols in these cards are usually accompanied by extraneous symbols, introduced by the various designers of the packs, that often differ from each other, sometimes becoming very idiosyncratic and confusing. Two colourful packs that adhere well to the true spirit of the major arcana are the Golden Dawn Pack and the Rider/Waite Pack. Both packs emerged from the practices of the Hermetic Order of the Golden Dawn, a mystery fraternity to which we return in the next section, that flourished in the late 19th and the early 20th centuries and that represented the first serious modern effort to bring the ancient mystery traditions together and synthesize them into a set of coherent disciplined practices for the conscious exploration of the inner realms of the mind. On the strength of these explorations the Golden Dawn developed a model of the mind that appealed not only to contemporary artists and men of letters, such as William Butler Yeats, contemporary scientists like Sir William Crookes, and to the Astronomer Royal for Scotland, William Peck, but to modern psychologists and psychotherapists, in particular those in the tradition of Carl Jung. This model drew heavily upon the Tarot and the Kabbalah among other sources, and those who dismiss the Tarot and its association with the archetypes as superstitious nonsense are almost invariably individuals who have never troubled to study either of these subjects in any depth.

Rosicrucianism and the Golden Dawn

After Christianity was adopted as the official religion of the Roman Empire in the fourth century CE, and identified in consequence with the power and authority of Rome, it took over Roman imperialistic thinking and claimed exclusive rights to the Keys to the Kingdom of Heaven. Hermetic practioners (including followers of the Gnostic traditions within Christianity itself), who believed that once initiated into the right meditation practices each person can find his or her own way, became subject to persecution, and in consequence kept their beliefs and their practices increasingly secret. It was not, in fact, until the 17th century that freedom of thought became generally possible, and it emerged that the Hermetic tradition was, and had been, kept alive not by the unlettered but by some of the finest minds of the time both in religion and in science. In addition, leading thinkers in the 17th century were now intent on asking questions about the nature of reality, of existence, of human destiny, and of the knowledge and practices that would allow the soul to rise above the trials and tribulations of material life, and were no longer content to accept everything on the authority of the Church.

A fresh growth of interest in the Hermetic tradition was also sparked off by the appearance in Strasbourg in 1616 of a very strange publication entitled in English translation *The Chemycal Wedding of Christian Rosenkreutz*. *The Chemycal Wedding* had been preceded by two other short publications, *The Fame of the Praiseworthy Order of the Rosy Cross* written in German and the *Confessio Fraternitas* written in Latin which told the story of a supposed occult adept, Christian Rosenkreutz, and the ancient fraternity that he founded which was devoted to healing and the advancement of knowledge and science through alchemical and geometrical truths. *The Chemycal Wedding* differed in that it was written as a romance involving a magical castle and the mystical marriage of the soul with the Divine by means of visions and initiation ceremonies. The adventure takes place over seven days, and the story is full of occult and alchemical imagery including death and resurrection and the magical creation of artificial life. The two earlier books had contained invitations to join what was described as the 'Invisible College' of the Rosicrucian Fraternity (or Brotherhood of the Rosy Cross). However, there is no record of anyone hearing from the fraternity or being taken into its membership, in spite of later claims that the physical body of Christian Rosenkreuz had actually been discovered miraculously preserved in a tomb decorated with magical and alchemical symbols.

In an age preoccupied by theology and the search for the miraculous, the three publications were taken very seriously, and before long, groups calling themselves Rosicrucians sprang up throughout Western Europe. Claims have since been made that Rosicrucianism dates back 1,500 years before the birth of Christ, and that Rosicrucians were involved in the building of the pyramids, in the birth of the Hermetic tradition, in Solomon's building of the Temple in Jerusalem, in the development of Freemasonry and the Order of the Knights Templar, and in many other occult movements. It makes an excellent story, and there are still groups in Europe and in America that claim to be the authentic descendants of Rosicrucianism and the guardians of its wisdom. However, it is now generally thought that all three publications were written by a German Lutheran pastor and theologian, Johann Valentin Andreae (1586–1654) partly to promote Protestant ethics and criticize the pope, and partly as a literary joke. One of the earlier works published in 1602 under his own name was actually entitled *Chemycal Wedding*, and apologies for the misleading effects of the three publications were written by the well-known English doctor and occultist William Fludd and by the German Count Michael Maier, counsellor to Emperor Rudolph the Second, both of whom are thought to have dabbled for a time in Rosicrucianism.

The whole thing then would seem to have been a joke on the part of Andreae. But was it? Firstly, if it were a joke, Andreae never admitted to it, and this at a time when his own Church, Lutheranism, was similar to Catholicism in its hostility to occultism and to those who appeared to dabble with the spirits. Secondly, the three publications, which amount to little more than slim pamphlets, had a profound effect not only upon Hermeticism but upon European thought in general, a rather unlikely result if they were no more than a joke. Together they helped lead to an orientation towards science and experiment that not only inspired the foundation of Hermetic fraternities like the Golden Dawn but even provided some impetus for the creation of the Royal Society and other respectable scientific societies. Was Andreae in fact an initiate into some shadowy fraternity than did indeed guard Hermetic secrets? And was the invitation to join the Rosicrucian Fraternity really an invitation to join, not a flesh and blood organization, but the 'Invisible College' to which the pamphlets referred? Was it in fact an invitation to take part in ways of thinking and practising that would lead to a uniform inner transformation? And was *The Chemycal Wedding*, in spite of its obscure symbolism, a manual on these ways of thinking and practising?

In discussing these historical matters we seem to have moved a long way from the practicalities of visualization. However, it is important to know something of the historical background of the subject for four reasons. Firstly, because history shows that since the earliest times of which we have any record visualization has played a vital and hugely formative role in human thought and behaviour. Secondly, because by learning a little of the history of the Hermetic tradition we gain an idea of the enduring strength of the tradition and of its influence upon Western thought. Thirdly, because the history of this tradition illustrates the extent to which it has been driven underground in the past by the hostility of Church leaders (a hostility that incidentally is now maintained by a modern scientific world view that takes account only of the material world and dismisses the idea of higher, non-physical realities). And fourthly, and perhaps most importantly, because many of the visualization techniques described in this book and that are now accepted as a means towards psychological and spiritual growth by transpersonal psychology and certain influential schools of counselling and psychotherapy, have their origin in the Hermetic tradition. Effectively, this tradition has done most to keep visualization practices alive in the West and to secure their use for present generations.

To these reasons we can add that the Hermetic tradition at its scholarly best has broadened our understanding of the potential of the human mind. Not only has it shown that the mind has extraordinary powers, it has demonstrated that these powers can be used to secure positive changes to a range of the individual's ways of relating to the self and to both seen and unseen realities. Its visualization and meditation practices bear close resemblance to those of Eastern psycho-spiritual traditions such as Hinduism and Buddhism, and it has demonstrated the psychological and spiritual power of symbols and of symbol systems, and the extraordinary strength of the human will when properly trained and applied. At no point should the Hermetic tradition be confused with human superstition and credulity, or with any of the more naïve so-called New Age movements. Like Eastern meditative and mind-expanding practices, it has, from the first, been deeply focused upon well-researched findings as well as upon extensive, if esoteric, scholarship. We have good reason to be grateful to the many men and women who, at risk to their lives, kept the tradition alive over the centuries.

Visualization and Modern Science

Science has been enormously successful in unravelling many of the practical questions about the material world, but there are many fundamental questions about ourselves and about the nature of reality that it cannot answer. One of these is the crucial question of the relationship between our mind and our brain. For centuries it was thought that mind and brain are separate, and that the mind is a non-physical entity – the soul or an aspect of the soul – that works through the body. Thus we *have* a body, rather than we *are* a body. However, the picture has now changed owing to modern advances in brain research. We now know which areas of the brain are activated when certain mental events take place, we have developed drugs that work upon the brain in order to change mental states, and we can probe the brain with electrodes that appear able to alter even deep-seated mental problems such as depression. Owing to these advances many scientists – neuropsychiatrists, neuropsychologists, neurologists – take the view that the mind is no more than a by-product of physical brain activity. Some even argue that the conscious mind is simply an accidental and largely unnecessary by-product of this activity, just as noise is an unnecessary but unavoidable by-product of the workings of the internal combustion engine.

This view is unwarranted. We know exactly why and how the internal combustion engine produces noise (which is itself a physical event) but, as I said earlier, we have no accurate idea how the physical, electrochemical activity of the brain can produce a non-physical phenomenon like the mind. We have never found the mind in the brain, and it is doubtful that we are any nearer to finding it now than we were at the beginning of modern brain research. Thus, the alternative hypothesis that the mind works *through* the brain rather than *because* of it makes equal sense, and is supported by the evidence from near-death experiences (Chapter 6) and from abilities such as telepathy and clairvoyance which indicate that the mind appears able to operate outside the constraints of the physical body, and indeed outside the limits of time and space that are the boundaries of our physical reality. This hypothesis has it that the brain is simply the interface between the non-physical mind and the physical body. It argues that the brain is bound to be active in response to instructions from the mind, just as the electric circuitry in a television set is rendered active by the signal sent to it from the television studio and the transmitter.

The importance of this mind-brain distinction will become clearer as we discuss the various functions of visualization throughout the book, and having touched upon it and completed this brief survey of the historical background to visualization, we are ready to begin to look at the practicalities. The simplest example of visualization, and the one most frequently practised by most of us, is memory. If I ask you to remember how your bedroom looks (assuming you are not reading this in bed!), you will usually have no difficulty in doing this. With your eyes closed to cut out the visual stimulation of your immediate environment, you will see in your mind's eye the details of the room. You can even scan it in memory, looking first towards the door and then around the walls and towards the window. We take this kind of experience so much for granted that we rarely pause to think what an extraordinary mental feat it actually happens to be. How is the mind able to conjure up this vision, so very clearly (if you are already a good visualizer) that it is almost as if you are actually in the room concerned?

There is a particular ability known as photographic memory – or more correctly 'eidetic imagery' – possessed by many children before the age of puberty, but only by some one per cent of adults that enables the above visualization exercise to be carried out so clearly that it is indeed as if one is actually in the room. Those who retain this ability into adulthood claim which in examinations, for example, they can answer questions by recalling the exact page in the textbook that deals with the issue concerned, and then 'reading' down the page until they find the details they want (students who are able to do this tell me that they feel rather guilty about it, as if they are cheating). Whether we are able to do it with the clarity of eidetic imagery or not, how is the mind able to store and recall visions of familiar places? We do not know. Similarly, how is it able to store and recall visual memories of certain events, such as a visit to the seaside when a child, or a sporting triumph or our first sight of a foreign country? Again, we do not know. Unlike a computer that stores information electronically by the simple expedient of binary processing we do not have a hard disc in our heads and the brain does not operate by binary processing. In addition, even when in a near-death or an out-of body experience we still carry our memories with us – for example we can recognize our surroundings and even our own bodies left behind in bed or wherever. But although we do not know how this miracle happens, we know that it does happen, and that most people can summon up visual memories virtually at will.

The Influence of the Mind on Physical Health

For much of the 20th century it was thought that the mind – whether inside the brain or outside – had little or no influence upon the health and well-being of the body. For health purposes, the mind and the body were considered as separate from each other. Times have changed. Now it is recognized, on good evidence, that the two are intimately linked, and that in fact at least one third of physical illnesses are connected in some way with our mental life, and the actual percentage may be even higher. We know, for example, that prolonged periods of stress appear to be a contributory factor in a number of ailments. And we know that traumatic life events, such as the death of a partner or a close relative, divorce, redundancy, financial problems and even moving house, are all associated with an increased incidence of physical illness in the subsequent two years. Thus, although the saying 'dying of a broken heart' may be something of an exaggeration, it does contain an element of truth.

If mental activity can sometimes make us physically ill, it makes sense to suppose it can also help keep us well and contribute to healing us when things go wrong. This is even more obvious if we turn to mental problems. It would be wrong to suppose that all such problems are self-imposed, but we can all too easily develop habits of thinking that are injurious to ourselves and very often to others. The most obvious of these is the way in which we think about our abilities, our appearance, our success or failure in life, our ability to form lasting and loving relationships and to get on with people, and our hopes and expectations for the future. One of the things that most dismayed me when I first became involved as a psychologist in counselling and psychotherapeutic work was the negative way in which people so often described themselves when telling me of their problems. If you think of yourself as foolish or stupid, as socially inadequate, as likely to make a mess of anything you undertake, as hopeless at relationships, as physically unattractive, and as generally something of a disaster, you are more than likely to turn these things into self-fulfilling prophecies – in other words you risk turning yourself into the very kind of person you are describing. This doesn't mean we should avoid being honest with ourselves. Self-honesty is one of the essential signs of maturity. But it does mean that we should be realistic, and recognize and emphasize the things we *can* do rather than the things we can't, the things we are good at rather than the things at which we feel a failure. And at the same time we should always recognize and emphasize our potential and our ability to improve. We may not be the best in the world at the things we hold dear, but we can certainly aspire to giving of our best.

The major cause of avoidable psychological problems is the inability to value ourselves. Valuing ourselves has nothing to do with conceit or self-aggrandizement. People who give the impression they think of themselves as a very special gift to humanity are often overcompensating for low self-esteem. It has everything to do with recognizing that we are each a unique human being, with far more potential for success than we ever realize. One of the secrets for realizing this potential is to *think* of ourselves as successful in whatever it is we set out to do. Another is to *see* ourselves as successful. We can do this either by imagining ourselves, from inside our heads as it were, achieving one of our goals such as doing well at a job interview, performing well in a sporting event, behaving easily and naturally at a social event. The other way is to observe ourselves as if from outside. This is much harder, but adds another dimension to a visualization exercise. It is a fact of life that we never, from the cradle to the grave, actually *see* ourselves. We can look down at our arms and hands, at our legs and feet and at the front of our bodies, but we can never see ourselves from the back or see our faces without using a mirror. Other people can see us as we never see ourselves. They can see us from every angle and every position. They know how we look much better than we do. But we can *visualize* ourselves. Why should seeing ourselves from outside help us to make more complete use of the powers of visualization? The answer is that it gives the unconscious more information with which to work. It confirms to the unconscious exactly what we want to happen, and confirms also that we are confident that success is possible. It doesn't – and this is important – try to tell the unconscious that success is *assured*. Believing that success is assured can lead to disappointment. If we expect visualization alone will enable us to achieve anything we want, against all the odds, we may only be disappointed, and end up feeling that visualization hasn't helped. Our message to the unconscious should be that we *expect* to do well.

Chapter 2

Visualization for Self-Transformation

Visualization and Physical Movement

To an important extent we are each of us our own creation. Certainly our genetic inheritance and our early experiences both play major roles in shaping the person we have become, but our way of thinking about ourselves also plays a major role, and the potential for bringing about psychological change in ourselves (mental and emotional) by changing aspects of this way of thinking, remains with us throughout our lives. Carl Jung, in fact, was adamant that our later years represent one of the most significant periods of our lives. By the time we reach these years we have been through all the various stages of growing up, childhood, adolescence, early adulthood and middle and late adulthood. We have encountered many of the most formative experiences that life has to offer – education, close emotional relationships, parenthood, career, bereavement on the death of grandparents and parents, travel, perhaps health and financial problems – with the result that the later years are a time for reflection, for making sense of life, and for thinking more deeply about who we are, where we came from, and ultimately where we are going when our time comes to leave.

However, the opportunities for influencing our own psychological development do not have to wait until we are in our mature years. Life is a miraculous gift. If you think about it, the strangest thing is that we should exist at all, and that we should be the unique individuals that we are. Throughout human history there has never been another individual exactly like you, either in natural gifts or in life experience. Even identical twins differ in subtle ways from each other as a result of occupying different positions in the womb during pregnancy and of the small genetic mutations that can take place during this time. Consequently, it is up to us to honour ourselves, and to do our best to realize our unique potential.

Body Image

How well do we know ourselves? Since this is a book about visualization, begin by exploring how you visualize yourself. We all have a body image, the result of seeing ourselves in mirrors, of the way we feel about our bodies, of the things others tell us about how we look, and of the extent to which we fall short of our ideal! Start the exploration by imagining you are doing some familiar task that involves movement, such as walking to the car, clearing the table, taking a shower, cutting the grass or climbing the stairs, but instead of being in your body imagine you are watching yourself from outside (Box 3 gives more details). What impression do you get, not just of how your body looks but of how you use it? Are your movements balanced and relaxed, or tense and ungainly? Do you look at home in your body or as if you are merely a visitor? If you were a stranger what would you deduce about this person just by watching? The people I have seen who are most at home in their bodies are Zen and T'ai Chi masters who move in a coordinated and unhurried way, without self-consciousness or wasted energy, as if they are at one with the space around them and movement and stillness flow effortlessly into each other. The secret lies not just in the master's body but in the mind. The mind is fully in the moment and in the movement, and there are no distractions pulling it first one way and then another. Even simple physical relaxation depends more than anything upon being aware of the body, so that the moment any tensions develop they can immediately be released.

We cannot all be Zen masters or T'ai Chi masters (and if you are one or the other you will certainly not need this book), but what are your reactions as you visualize yourself in movement? Are there signs of stress and tension, of mind and body pulling in different directions, of a sense that your mind is not in your actions? Now look at your body image, objectively and without any attempt at self-congratulation or self-rejection. As a follow-up, and particularly if you have found this visualization difficult, you can

---

Box 3: Seeing Yourself from Outside

Visualizing yourself from outside does not come easily (though as we shall see in Chapter 6 it is one of the methods used to induce out-of-body experiences). If you find it particularly difficult, ask someone to make a video or a DVD of you carrying out a routine task. Watch the video or the DVD until you get some idea of how you look. At the same time take careful notice of your surroundings. If you are not using a video or a DVD decide on what surroundings to use so that you can commit them to memory.

Sit comfortably, as in the first two exercises, close your eyes and focus on your breathing for a minute or two, then visualize these surroundings. When the visualization is established, put your own image into the picture. Don't worry about getting the details of your face exactly right. Just watch your movement as you go about the routine task which you have set yourself.

Keep up the visualization as long as feels comfortable.

---

watch yourself in a mirror. To help your visualization skills try closing your eyes for a moment while watching yourself, as if you are taking a photograph, and allow the movement you have just been watching to continue behind your closed eyelids as if in a video. Do this several times. The vision will usually remain reasonably clear for a short time, and then fade. You certainly do have powers of visualization. They just need practice.

What did you learn from this exercise? Remember that the secret of the relaxed, coordinated movement that avoids tensions and wasted effort (one of the reasons we often feel unnecessarily tired after completing certain tasks is that tensions squander energy) lies not just in the body but in the mind. If you 'saw' yourself in the exercise as awkward and as unlike a Zen or a T'ai Chi master as you could be, then you have demonstrated to yourself there is a need to develop better body awareness and to put your mind into the moment rather than wasting it in distractions. And what did you learn about your body image? Were you positive or negative about yourself? Taking both movement and body image together, what are your conclusions about yourself? One of the aids to good physical health is the ability to feel well about ourselves. Not vain or narcissistic, but affectionate and friendly towards our own bodies. After all, they do an awful lot for us. The body, as the Bible tells us, is indeed the temple of the spirit, and it is up to us to be grateful to it and to care for it, rather than to be destructively self-rejecting, or to be influenced by fashion into torturing it in an attempt to turn it into something that it is not.

Now let's try another part of this visualization exercise. Having watched yourself as you imagine you are, try watching yourself moving without all the tensions and the wasted effort. Close your eyes, then select the imaginary activity that you used before, and watch yourself moving calmly and with your mind focused upon what you are doing. Typically when we are doing mundane tasks (and especially when we are engaged in tasks that we dislike) our minds are elsewhere, daydreaming of all the many things we would prefer to be doing or worrying about other unloved tasks waiting to be done.

Look again at Box 3 if necessary to remind yourself how to carry out this exercise, then close your eyes and begin. Notice the difference between this visualization and the last one. Notice first of all how the person you are visualizing is much more centred upon the activities being carried out and how much more fluid, graceful and economical his or her movements are, how much more coordinated the different parts of the body appear to be, as if working with each other and not against each other. Notice how much more efficient and effective the movements are, and how much more at home the person appears to be in the body. Then look at the body image. Does the person seem to be more comfortable and at ease with the body, more self-accepting and more in harmony with who he or she is? Do the qualities that appeared negative to you in the first visualization now seem much less so?

What are your conclusions this time? Were you happier with yourself and more self-accepting? Were there as many things about yourself that you wished to change this time? Whatever your conclusions, simply note them. This is only work in progress. The first part of this exercise need only be completed once. From then on, concentrate upon the second part, making it a regular feature of your visualization meditation. Like all visualizations, keep it relatively simple. Focus upon yourself as relaxed, balanced and undistracted, with a pleasing body image. Don't spend too long on the exercise each time. Frequency is more important than duration. Use it for two or three minutes as an effective way of centring yourself and calming yourself at the start of each meditation session, particularly if you meditate in the evening and the day has been particularly hectic and stressful.

Visualization and Stillness

Many of the points that apply to movement apply also to stillness. The ability to be still is an essential part of meditation. Whether watching television or sitting at a desk or waiting for a train many people find it difficult to remain still. They also have problems with silence, largely because the frantic, noisy world in which we live shortens our attention span and conditions us to feel uncomfortable unless we are surrounded by constant activity and loud noise. Television bombards us with rapidly changing (often violent) images, and mindless blaring music confronts us almost every time we enter a shop or a restaurant. This unrelenting diet of activity and noise encourages superficiality of both thinking and feeling. We are rarely given the space to go deeply into anything, least of all ourselves.

Visualization exercises can help us feel more at home with stillness and silence. There is no need first to visualize yourself unable to sit still. You will probably be already well aware that you have a problem here. Instead, concentrate on visualizing yourself sitting in meditation with the calm, unmoving presence of a Zen master. If this visualization proves too difficult, sit before a mirror, watching yourself carefully and thinking of yourself centred by the gravity of the earth beneath you and by a silken thread connecting you to the sky above. When this image is stabilized, close your eyes and focus upon holding it as a visualization.

Zen Buddhism has many metaphors for the way one should sit in meditation, but most of them stress this fact of *presence*. One is simply present, here and now, in this particular time and place, unmoving and still. The present moment is all we have. And just as one is present in time and place, so one is present in one's own mind. In the stillness and silence of meditation there is nowhere else to be. This is the reality of the moment. Nothing is allowed to pull the attention away from this sense of being present, of being fully and entirely who and what one is. Without artificial concepts about what is real and what is not, one simply experiences the act of *being*. Except in meditation, how rarely are we aware of just *being*! Usually we are too busy talking to other people or to ourselves, and language – for all its great beauty and its marvellous ability to communicate meaning – often comes between us and being. Even when we are not talking, we are still using language to chatter away to ourselves. The result is that language often distances us from the direct experience of being alive. Meditation

---

Box 4: Sitting Meditation

Many readers of this book will be very familiar with stillness meditation, but for those who are less sure about it there are a few simple rules. These rules represent what we might call the basic structure of meditation practice. All other forms of meditation, including visualization meditation, build upon them in ways that will become increasingly clear as we go through the book.

1. All meditation involves focused *attention*. The meditator *attends* to a chosen stimulus. When thoughts arise they are ignored. If the mind does become caught up in them and wanders away it is brought gently back.

2. The most widely used practice focuses attention upon the breathing. The meditator becomes aware of the cool feeling in the nose on the in-breath and the warm feeling on the out-breath.

3. By attending to the stimulus and refusing to become lost in thought, the mind gradually becomes still. Mind and body become peaceful and at rest.

4. This peace is the natural state of the mind. This is what the mind and what pure being actually are.

5. As the meditator becomes more experienced so this peace becomes a part of daily life, and the meditator is much better able to withstand the stresses and strains that life brings.

---

and the use of visualization help free us from this overreliance on the spoken word, and allow us to rest tranquilly in the present (see Box 4).

Visualizing yourself sitting in meditation conveys to the unconscious that this is how you wish to be, and that this is your true nature. Our thoughts and our emotions, our doing and our getting, are temporary events that come and go, and although of value in themselves, we must not deceive ourselves into thinking they are who we are. There is a time to make use of them and a time to let them rest and to return to ourselves.

When visualizing yourself in sitting meditation always see yourself in the same clothes. If possible keep some items of clothing – such as a dressing gown, a track suit or a shawl – specifically for use in all forms of meditation, whether visualization meditation or sitting meditation. The act of putting them on will help turn your mind towards meditation. In the same way, keep a special cushion or a special upright chair for meditation, and try if you can to sit in the same place and at the same time each day. If other commitments mean that that a special time or place is not possible, then work just when you can. But keeping to a regular programme is likely to lead to quicker progress. Essentially what you are doing in your visualization practice is training your unconscious to help you achieve your goals, whether these are physical, psychological or spiritual. And, as with any training, regularity and a degree of dedication are important. Your unconscious will have become quite set in its habits, owing primarily to the fact that, like most of us, you have not realized its importance and the need to be in proper communication with it. As a result it has been allowed to go its own way, and re-educating it to understand what is required of it is going to take a little time.

Visualizations for Specific Psychological Problems

Psychologists have found that visualization can be a very effective way of helping people troubled by high anxiety levels, whether the anxiety is irrational (for example phobias such as the fear of going out or of confined spaces) or rational (such as attacks of nerves before examinations, job interviews or public speaking engagements). High anxiety levels are a major problem for many people, and can handicap their behaviour and their performance in a number of radical ways. A calm, relaxed mind is much better at assessing if fears are rational or irrational, and in organizing one's thinking and recall during exams or other stressful events. The body also performs much better at a wide range of tasks if we are not too nervous. An attack of nerves is a symptom that the body is gearing up to run away from what it regards as a threatening situation, and if it is unable to do so the nervousness gets worse and reaches the point where it has an inhibiting or even incapacitating effect upon our attempts to tackle the challenge facing us. Telling ourselves not to be nervous is of limited use. The body is already pumping adrenalin and noradrenalin into the bloodstream, and increasing heart rate and blood pressure by anything up to 50 per cent. The energy that should be used to escape from the threatening situation ends up like a damned stream, causing hands to shake, limbs to tremble, memory to fail, the voice to become hoarse and the words inarticulate.

So the ability to relax at stressful times is invaluable, and this is where visualization meditation can come in. Many of us have minor irrational anxieties, like fear of the dentist (despite the fact that toothache is far worse), fear of flying (regardless of the fact that flying is the safest form of travel) or of snakes (though snakes are not slimy, are pleasant to hold, and the chances of meeting a poisonous one in Europe are very small). Such anxieties, though by no means as incapacitating as the phobias mentioned above, can be highly inconvenient, and visualization offers a readily available way of helping deal with them. Even people with extreme irrational phobic anxieties, that require the help of trained psychologists and psychotherapists, can use visualizations to supplement professional treatment. The procedure, whether the irrational anxiety is minor or phobic, involves recognizing that the unconscious needs to be reprogrammed to view the supposedly threatening situation in a more realistic and acceptable light. And it will by now come as no surprise to learn that the most effective way to start this reprogramming is by visualizing yourself engaging in this situation as if it is *not* threatening. Thus, depending on the nature of the problem, you visualize yourself visiting the dentist or flying above the clouds or actually handling snakes in a perfectly relaxed and confident way.

You may protest that you can't do this, as the very thought of the threatening situation throws you into a panic. If this is the case, the answer is to proceed gradually, following the procedure detailed below for rational anxieties. The unconscious – which, with the autonomic nervous system, is after all responsible for your nerves – cannot be reprogrammed at one go. Like most learning tasks, such reprogramming is best done in stages. We can illustrate this by detailing how to work with a rational anxiety such as the fear of examinations. The visualization programme is best started some days (some weeks if necessary) before the examination is actually due to take place. Starting early, before the examination is close enough to seem threatening, allows one to go through a number of sessions of visualization until one is finally able to visualize the examination itself while remaining in a properly relaxed state. All too often we try to put thoughts of threatening situations out of our minds every time such thoughts intrude, with the result that we never properly prepare ourselves emotionally. No matter how much revision we have done for the examination, we still haven't been preparing for the stress of the event itself, that is for walking into the examination room and taking our seat, looking for the first time at the examination paper, and marshalling our thoughts.

The important thing is to be properly relaxed at the start of each of these sessions, so a few minutes should be spent sitting quietly and focusing on the breathing (Box 4). Once you are reasonably relaxed, which means being able to give yourself a score of at least 7 on a scale of 1 to 10, you are ready to start visualizing, in as much detail as possible, all that takes place on the day of the examination before you finally sit down at your desk in the examination room. The starting point will be when you awake on the morning of the examination (or even when you go to bed the previous evening if you think you will have trouble sleeping). Visualize yourself waking, and taking in all the details of the bedroom as you open your eyes. Then visualize going through the subsequent events of the morning (getting up, showering, dressing, breakfasting etc.), remaining relaxed all the time. If you feel at any point that tension is rising and that your score on the 10-point scale is slipping below 7, stop the exercise and focus upon relaxing again. Once you are relaxed, go back to the beginning of the exercise and start again. It doesn't matter if you feel rather bored. Strange as it may seem, boredom can actually be a help. Once we are bored with an activity it loses much of its power to make us nervous. We can even become bored with our own nerves, which also helps convey the message to the unconscious that nerves are not that important after all.

Don't forget to visualize as much detail as you can at each point. It is of little use to try and skim through the day. Unless you pay attention to detail you are not really relating to the experience at all. You need to make everything as close to reality as possible. Continue the visualization exercise by going through the events of the day until you reach a point where you find it difficult to keep your score as high as 7, even if you try several times. This is the time to stop. The next occasion you try the exercise you will find it easier to get past this point. When you find you are able to get some way before the anxiety starts to build, there is no need to go back to the beginning every time. Just return part of the way to the time before you began to feel tense.

Practise the visualization as often as you can – every day if possible. The aim is to imagine going right through to the examination room and starting to write without feeling too nervous. A little excited perhaps – which can help stimulate the rush of ideas – but not disabled by nerves. If it is possible to enter the examination room before the date of the examination, when the room is empty and you can sit there and relax, this is a great help not only in your ability to visualize the room, but to experience being there without nerves. This is equally important if the occasion that causes anxiety is not an examination but public speaking. I always advise those who have to give a lecture or a speech, or speak in public for any reason, to go into the room concerned when it is empty, to stand up on the platform and imagine the empty chairs full of people while you focus upon relaxing. I still do this myself before giving a talk or lecture of any kind. From experience over the years I have found this a great help in putting myself at ease during the actual event.

Visualization for Social Self-Confidence

In the above exercises you are not only calming your nerves, you are also building up your confidence. You are visualizing yourself not only remaining calm but succeeding at the task you have set yourself. This is true even if your problem has nothing to do with high-profile events such as examinations or public speaking. If the problem is how to feel relaxed in ordinary social situations, the visualization procedure is still much the same, although there may be no need to go through all the details leading up to the event. It may be enough simply to visualize entering the social gathering, seeing the people chatting together, and experiencing yourself as relaxed and free from the inaccurate but common feeling that everyone is looking at you. Don't focus on yourself but on your surroundings, which helps avoid self-consciousness. Remain relaxed, and visualize yourself looking people in the face and smiling. A smile is always the best introduction. Don't visualize yourself as making a great effort to shine or to break into other people's conversations. It is enough to be there and to feel at ease. Only join in the talk when there is a pause and you have something useful to contribute. Remember that one of the best ways of joining in is simply to listen, showing interest in what is being said. And provided they are not intrusive, asking relevant questions of whomever is speaking is one of the best ways of becoming part of a group.

If you start feeling socially uncomfortable at any point in the visualization then, as with the examination exercise, pause until you feel at ease again, then go back to where you began and start afresh. As with all visualization exercises, don't expect difficulties to be solved overnight. Embarrassment in social situations typically goes back to early childhood experiences, when you may have been unkindly criticized or made fun of by adults or other children. In addition, you are probably rather sensitive by nature, anxious to please and to be liked and accepted. Maybe you have also grown up overconcerned about your appearance and your body image, or fearful you have nothing interesting to say, or that you lack the confidence to tell amusing stories, or are unable to act naturally with the opposite sex. Whatever the reason, the problem needs working on regularly through visualizations. Note every improvement as it happens. Even small improvements soon add up to a major advance. Remember also that each social situation is different. Keep in mind that you are not merely making your social life easier, you are actually changing something important about yourself. As you grow in self-confidence in social situations, so you grow in confidence about yourself, and with that comes a growth in self-esteem, an essential factor in psychological health.

Irrational fears are tackled in much the same way, by a series of visualizations of the circumstances leading up to the visit to the dentist or to catch the plane or whatever. In every case, the aim is to see yourself carrying out the visit or the task concerned success-fully and confidently and with a low anxiety level. The secret is to do it in gentle, easy stages spread over however many days you wish, and only getting to the point where you visualize the actual event itself when you can do so while remaining relaxed. Patience and practice are vital. Even with a phobia such as a fear of open spaces (*agoraphobia*), which can be so severe in some cases that one is afraid to leave the house, the procedure is again to visualize oneself succeeding in easy stages. The first stage might be visualizing oneself opening the front door and standing in the porch. When this can be done while remaining relaxed, the next stage might be leaving the porch and standing on the garden path, the next one walking to the front gate and so on. As each of these stages becomes established, so one can carry out the action in real life. Thus, when one can visualize standing in the porch and feeling comfortable one can feel confident enough actually to do it.

With the opposite phobia, the fear of enclosed spaces (*claustrophobia*) one might choose to start by visualizing being alone in a large room, and closing the windows and the doors (or only some of them if this seems difficult at first). The next stage might be to visualize a smaller room, perhaps with one other person there. Finally, by easy stages, one is ready to visualize entering a lift, or being in a crowd of people. If the phobia is perhaps to do with snakes, one can start by visualizing a very small harmless snake in a glass aquarium, and eventually progress to watching (or even handling) a large (though still harmless!) one. Even depression and low spirits can be helped to improve through visualization. Here the procedure is to break the habit (and it can indeed become a habit) of thinking of ourselves as low spirited by imagining what it would be like to be happy. We can visualize ourselves in a happy space, of the kind described below when we talk about stress, doing the things we like doing, enjoying these things free of the psychological weight that has been dragging us down. A few minutes each day, particularly in the morning, spent in visualizations of this kind begin to tell the unconscious that this is not only how we want to be but how we actually can be. Over time, it absorbs and responds to the message.

Visualization *is* effective in helping us cope with anxieties, rational or otherwise, and difficulties such as depression, provided we want to make it work and are prepared to give it the necessary time and patience. A word of caution, however. Anxieties are strange things. Some people become unconsciously attached to their own, either because anxieties, even though uncomfortable, can nevertheless become part of our identity (part of who we think we are) which makes them hard to relinquish, or because they can be used as attention-seeking devices with family and friends. It is no bad idea to look at our anxieties to see if they come into these categories. Probably they do not, but if they do they can be a hindrance to progress until we recognize what is going on, and unburden ourselves of such unnecessary psychological baggage.

Visualization for Stress Reduction

While life in the West has become increasingly free from the scourges that plagued mankind for many centuries – famine, disease, poverty and physical danger – so it has become more, rather than less, stressful. Stress, caused by the pressures we put upon ourselves in our careers and family lives along with the pressures a frantic, noisy and polluted modern environment imposes upon us, is now both a psychological and a physical threat to the very well-being that we strive so hard to achieve. To these pressures can be added the vacuum caused by the decline in spiritual values and, with this decline, a loss of ultimate meaning and purpose to life. Taken together these various causes of stress can rob life of its intrinsic joy, and the mind and body of energy enthusiasm and good health.

Meditation is one of the very best antidotes to these pressures. In meditation the mind returns to itself instead of being pulled in all directions by the demands and distractions of the outside world. Having returned to itself, it discovers that its natural state is calm and peaceful, alert and attentive, and free from the distractions that occupy so much of our time. Meditation techniques such as focusing upon the breathing (Box 4) are excellent at taking us to this untroubled place within ourselves, and introducing visualizations into a meditation programme can be a further major benefit. When using visualization, focus upon a place, real or imaginary, associated with peace and tranquillity, a place where you can feel happy. It can be a place in the countryside or in the mountains or by the sea or a river. Decide for yourself what is most appropriate for you. Some people like to visualize the inside of a great cathedral, while others prefer a vast art gallery, or a small cottage in the countryside. Whatever you choose, return to the same place in each meditation. Think of it as somewhere welcoming and peaceful where you can go whenever you please. You may prefer to visualize it as if seen through closed eyes, or you may prefer to think of it as on a screen between and just above your eyes (the so-called 'third eye' used as a point of focus by some Eastern meditative traditions). The whole visualization may come to you easily, or you may prefer to build it up, item by item. For example, if you choose to be at the seaside or on a tropical island, start by looking out to sea, watching the sun sparkle on the waves and the waves break on the shore. Then widen your vision and see the wide expanse of the beach with its soft sand, and the trees bordering the beach moving gently in the breeze. You can 'see' the beach as deserted, or you may prefer to see people in the distance, enjoying the sunshine, tranquil and peaceful as the scene itself.

Whatever you choose to visualize, avoid making it too animated. The purpose of the meditation is to calm things down, and allow you to become part of the tranquillity of the scene before you. Visualize it as a place where you feel safe and at ease, somewhere that belongs to you, free from unwanted intrusions, that revitalizes you and fills you with the strength to carry on with daily life. And when you close the visualization don't end it too abruptly, like turning off a light switch. Withdraw from it gently, knowing that it is always there to welcome you. Imagine the scene becoming gradually faint, as if a fine veil is being drawn over it. Then when it disappears, stay for a few moments with the space that it leaves behind, and feel the sense of relaxed peace that now exists. Feel grateful to the visualization (in all this work, as in life itself, gratitude is one of the most valuable of emotions), and say a few words of thanks.

Some people ask whether it is useful to use the other senses to help with the visualization. Should you for example imagine the sound of music if you are in a cathedral, or the sound of the waves if you are on the beach? And should you use the sense of touch, feeling the warm sand under your bare feet, or the lapping of the waves? The answer is *by all means*, as long as you do not allow the various sensations to become confused with each other or to distract you from the scene itself.

Visualization practices can also be used to help with specific experiences that may be causing you stress, such as problems with colleagues or with tight deadlines at work. As with the practices for helping you overcome examination nerves or lack of self-confidence in social situations, the secret is to build up a careful visualization of the experience concerned and the events leading up to it. As with the previous practices, aim to remain relaxed while working through the visualization. If you find undue anxieties beginning to arise, stop the visualization, concentrate upon relaxing once more, and when you feel sufficiently calm begin to build it up again.

Visualization for Career Goals

Career goals should be matched to one's interests, abilities and likely opportunities. However, once these realistic goals are identified, they should always be thought of as attainable. 'I can and I will' is a much better attitude than 'maybe I can' or, worst of all, 'maybe I can't'. Remember that this positive attitude does not have to be fiercely impressed upon your unconscious. Quiet confidence conveys a more effective message than gritted teeth determination. Paradoxically the latter indicates to the unconscious that the conscious mind is the one that is going to do the work. Of course one cannot leave it all to the deeper self. Part of the secret is for the conscious and unconscious areas of the mind to work together, the former acting as the creator and initiator and the latter as the executive who puts things into practice.

Make sure your visualizations remain realistic. We cannot predict the exact circumstances that will surround career success, and attempts at being too specific may lead to disappointment. Focus instead upon the things that symbolize for you the kind of success you want to achieve. For example, if you hope to become a writer, visualize books with your name on the spine, or magazines or newspapers with your name at the head of articles. If you want to become a successful architect, visualize the kind of building you would like to design. If you want to work in the law or in medicine, visualize the interior of a law court or of a healing centre. As these are symbols there is no need for them to have a contemporary look about them. It is the idea of becoming a writer, an architect or whatever that matters, and the symbol should stand for something that can represent this achievement. For example, a leather-covered book may be a better representation of literary success than a modern softback, an ancient Greek temple rather than a modern office block. Something that resonates deeply with you is more likely to impress your ambition and your determination upon your unconscious than something chosen simply because it presents a modern image. Although personal to you, rather than archetypal, these symbols are the language of your unconscious, and therefore serve as keys back into it. The unconscious immediately recognizes their meaning, and the need to help you satisfy your ambition.

Like all visualizations, those for career goals should be practised frequently. Eventually this leads to a point where they become an automatic accompaniment to any thoughts about future ambitions.

People vary greatly in these ambitions. Some are concerned primarily with themselves, while others think more in terms of service to the community. Some wish to work with their hands, others with their heads. Some prefer the idea of working with people, others prefer to work on their own. Some prefer the attractions of science and technology, others the attractions of the arts. Some see their chosen profession as an essential part of their identity, others regard it more as a way of making a living. But no matter in which of these various categories you happen to fall, the essential is to believe in your own success. No matter whether you have faith that self-belief draws unseen universal forces to your assistance or whether you think it helps you make better use of your own efforts, the important factor is that by impressing upon your unconscious that you have confidence in your career goals your chances of achieving them are immeasurably improved. There is nothing new about this. In the New Testament the Bible speaks of the fact that faith can 'remove mountains' (Corinthians 13:2), and throughout history all the great spiritual traditions – which are also profound psychological teachings long predating modern scientific psychology – have made it clear that faith brings results. However, like the New Testament, all stress that unless faith is accompanied by generosity towards fellow beings there is little virtue in one's achievements, whatever they may be.

Chapter 3

Visualization and Sporting Success

Sports Psychology

In 1975 Timothy Gallwey published the bestseller, *The Inner Game of Tennis*, in which he drew attention to the role the mind plays in whether or not we are able to reach our potential in a game such as tennis. He followed up with *The Inner Game of Golf*, and shortly afterwards founded The Inner Game Corporation designed to develop inner-game approaches to playing music, selling goods, managing businesses, handling stress and even dieting. Gallwey's work provided an important impetus for the development of sports psychology, i.e. the application of psychological principles to sporting performance. Sports psychology has proved so successful that now many professional footballers, athletes, golfers, cricketers, baseball players, in fact sportsmen and women in most fields of endeavour, consult sports psychologists in order to enhance their results. Top football and other clubs carry sports psychologists on their permanent staff, as do top golfers who are well aware that, as the old golfing saying has it, 'the most important hole is the one between the ears', meaning of course the mind.

Parallel with the interest in the inner-game approach has come an increasing emphasis in sport upon the so-called art of gamesmanship or mind games, in which one uses psychological strategies that remain within the rules yet nevertheless inhibit opponents' performance. The most extreme example is the attempt in high-concentration sports to distract opponents by time-wasting tactics or by slighting remarks at the very moment when they need to remain particularly focused. Gamesmanship is not unknown even in a highly intellectual game like chess. At a world chess championship some years ago one of the players had a supposed psychic among his support team who spent each game staring fixedly at the opponent amidst rumours that he was able to confuse the latter's thought processes.

I am certainly not advocating these profoundly unfair practices that do much to destroy the once honourable concept of sportsmanship. I mention them because they illustrate the point that nerves can seriously inhibit the performance of even top sportsmen and women. Gamesmanship is designed to upset opponents, to make them nervous and unsure of themselves, and all too often it succeeds. By contrast, the inner-game approach is all to do with triumphing over oneself, over one's nerves, over the attempt by the conscious mind to run things instead of allowing the unconscious to play its part. Following on from this, sports psychology is about putting ourselves in the right frame of mind to give of our best. Much that has already been said in Chapter 2 about using visualization to help in dealing with nerves applies equally to sport, but there are important additional things to be kept in mind. The first is that sport should be about fun, win or lose, but we in the West have largely lost our ability to view it as a light-hearted, non-serious activity. Vast amounts of money are now ploughed into (and made from) sport, and failure can prove very costly indeed. Along with money goes prestige and public image, since success and failure at the top level is played out in front of a television audience of millions. The trickle-down effect of this win-at-all-costs attitude is apparent now even in amateur sport. The competitive instinct has always been there of course, but now winning has become more important than competing, and the idea of enjoyment has been sacrificed.

Inevitably, the result is that sport has all too often become a highly stressful activity, and one way in which sports psychology tries to handle this is to help players visualize themselves not only playing confidently, but remaining calm and retaining their self-confidence even after making the errors that are inseparable from playing any game. The successful sportsman or woman is the person who makes an error and quickly puts it out of the mind in order to focus upon what happens next. We see this if we watch top golfers and top tennis players. The golfer may miss a crucial putt at an important hole, and the tennis player may lose a game in which he or she held match points. Top players, however, do not dwell upon what might have been. The last hole and the last game are already in the past. Worrying about them (or 'still carrying them' as it is sometimes called) when faced with the challenge of the next hole or the next game is a sure way to court another failure. This is so often the point at which some players go to pieces. They are said to 'choke' as nerves get in the way. Just as success breeds success so failure breeds failure. The hands tremble and become slippery with sweat, and the player goes on to beat him or herself, with a consequent loss of self-confidence that may play further upon the nerves in the future.

In the event of these and other problems it is productive to go back after the game is over and visualize what should have happened rather than what did happen. Dwelling on mistakes and failure does not help. Focusing on how to put them right certainly does. The latter may involve visualizing the physical actions that would have avoided the mistakes, or visualizing oneself undertaking these actions in a better frame of mind. Many golfers complain that after a time they develop slight tremors when taking a crucial putt, while track and field athletes sometimes speak of a 'mental barrier' that seems almost like a physical weight that holds them back at crucial moments. The relevant visualization involves going back over the moments when these problems occurred, and seeing oneself free of the handicaps that led to them.

Such handicaps are entirely mental in origin. There is nothing in the body that decides a golfer's hands should develop tremors when taking a putt, or that an unseen barrier should hold the athlete back at crucial moments during competition. The problem starts in the mind, and comes essentially from a fear of failure. In psychological terms what happens is that the unconscious has been 'taught' by the fears of the conscious mind to anticipate what is the worst thing that could happen at this moment. The worst thing, of course, is that one should miss the putt or fail to get the run-up to the high jump correct or to get into one's stride at the start of a sprint race. Having anticipated the worst thing, the unconscious mind then obligingly invents a way of making it happen. Because of its power – for bad as well as for good – over the body, the unconscious proceeds to cause tremors in the hands or to prevent the precise coordination necessary between the legs and the rest of the body.

The remedy is to 'teach' the unconscious that it must anticipate the best that can happen at the crucial moment instead of the worst. And as is so often the case, the best way for this teaching to be effective is not simply giving the unconscious a verbal message, but showing it, through visualization, what it must do next time. Thus the golfer visualizes the hands and arms moving smoothly through the putt, while the athlete visualizes the fluent and precise run-up to the bar and the sprinter visualizes the correct pick-up and stride pattern at the start and throughout the race. As always with visualization, these procedures must be carried out when the mind is fully relaxed. Anxiety in the conscious mind simply reinforces the negative message that the worst thing possible is going to happen. A relaxed and confident mind reinforces the positive message that the best thing is going to happen. The difference between the two scenarios could hardly be greater.

Handling Disasters as well as Triumphs

For this reason, sports psychology stresses the importance of visualizing not only success, but how to react when things don't go so well. Similar visualizations are equally important in all walks of life. Most of us find it difficult to handle unexpected setbacks, even minor ones like the sudden rudeness of a shop assistant, the failure of our computer at a crucial moment, and the bullying behaviour of another motorist on the drive home. Such setbacks are a fact of life, and the more sensitive we are, the more likely we are to be hurt by them, often out of all proportion to their seriousness. But no matter how often we tell ourselves to take them in our stride, we seem unable to do so. However, by visualizing ourselves succeeding, and thus imaginatively *living through* the incident without allowing it to upset or anger us, or lower our self-confidence, we once again demonstrate to the unconscious not only that this is how we want to be, but that (and this is what makes it so effective) this is how we can be.

You can visualize an actual incident that has upset you recently, or think up a typical scenario. Even a few short visualization sessions can prove very effective, particularly as the memory of them frequently comes back when faced with relevant situations in the future. But, like all visualization exercises, care must be taken to work through them methodically, building up and taking in all the details, even of the events leading up to the actual incident itself. It is of little use simply to attempt a rushed few minutes of half-visualized activity and expect to get results. Clarity and detail as always are essential.

Visualization – A Key to Good Judgement

There is another form of visualization that is vital in sport. Think of a top golfer about to play a stroke intended to land the ball as near as possible to the flag. He or she may know the distance to the flag, and may know the right club to use, but the margin between success and failure is all too narrow. Hit the ball a little too hard and it will run off the back of the green and into the rough. Hit it not quite hard enough and it will drop short, and roll into one of the bunkers guarding the green. Hit it a little to the right or to the left and it will go into the rough. With all this in mind, how can the golfer consciously judge the *exact* degree of strength needed to get the ball near the flag, and the *exact* angle at which the club head must hit the ball in order to keep it straight? The answer is that even a top golfer cannot. Past experience will play an important part but only a part, and it is here that visualization and the unconscious come into the picture. Notice how, before hitting the ball, he or she will look down at the ball, up at the flag, down at the ball, up at the flag a number of times before playing the stroke. Whether consciously or unconsciously, the golfer is visualizing the ball travelling in exactly the right direction and at the right speed and trajectory to end up at the flag. In response, the unconscious understands what is required, and takes over the final responsibility. The more practised the golfer is at this type of visualization, the more likely it is that the ball will end up where it should. The same mental preparation is also practised in other sports where the aim is to bring two objects close together. In bowls and in curling the player has to release the ball or the curling stone with just the right amount of force to take it close to (or where necessary actually hit) the target ball or stone. Again, the conscious mind cannot calibrate the exact amount of physical force to use. The player visualizes the shot he or she wishes to play, and the unconscious adjusts the actions of the body accordingly.

Take a different kind of example. Watch a top high jumper before beginning the run-up to the bar. He or she is clearly going through a rehearsal, visualizing each stride of the run-up, visualizing the moment when the body will twist slightly to put itself at the correct angle to the bar, and visualizing the body clearing the bar and landing safely on the other side. The same kind of mental preparation is necessary for the pole-vaulter and for the hurdler. Watch the hurdler waiting at the start of the 110-metres hurdles, a race in which the winning margin is so small that the slightest misjudgement can mean the difference between first and last. He or she gazes intently down the track, lost in concentration, visualizing the stride pattern to the first hurdle and between each of the hurdles, visualizing the split second of each take-off and the body clearing each hurdle, and then dipping as it crosses the finishing line. The 100-metre runner carries out an equally precise visualization – the moment of rising from the starting blocks, the number of strides before the body is fully upright, the subsequent focus upon the finishing line, and the effort needed for the body to reach it before the other runners. Sometimes referred to as 'tunnel vision', the runner shuts out the possible distractions presented by the athletes on either side and by the sound of the crowd. All that matters is the visualized tunnel down which he or she will run.

In all these examples visualization can be external and/or internal. Externally the golfer is visualizing the flight of the ball and the athlete the number of strides to the high jump bar or the first hurdle, while internally they are each focusing upon the action of the body as it swings the club or covers the ground. However, the two forms of visualization are really a single imaginative experience. Everything leads up to the point where *action follows imagination*. It is as if imagination has mapped out the path of the ball or of the body, and action then obediently follows this path.

Whatever sport interests you, watch top-class performers going through their various visualization routines. In cricket, the batsman at the wicket practising a shot is concerned not only with the feel of the bat in his hands but with the visualization of the ball coming off the blade and speeding to the boundary. The goalkeeper standing in the goalmouth waiting for the kick-off is visualizing the ball coming towards him and his perfect positioning as he moves to intercept it. The diver on the high board is preparing mentally

Box 5: Letting it Happen

Timothy Gallwey in *The Inner Game of Tennis* stresses that visualization should be followed by an attitude of mind that *lets* the desired result arise rather than tries to *make* it happen.

As an example, he suggests that if you are a tennis player you should put a marker in the service court on the other side of the net then attempt to hit it with the service ball, calculating in advance exactly how you should hold and swing the racket, the angle at which the racket should hit the ball and the degree of power behind it. Keep trying until the marker is hit, then try to repeat exactly the same actions in order to hit it again. A difficult task. This is trying to make it happen.

Next, he suggests visualizing the path of the ball from the racket to the marker. Repeat the visualization until the marker is hit every time. Then, without trying to hit the marker, ask the body (we would say instruct the unconscious) to do it for you. If you fail, don't try to correct the mistake, simply try again. Allow the body to make the corrections, and watch it doing so. This is *letting* it happen.

Letting it happen is far more effective than trying to *make* it happen. *Letting* it happen is *letting yourself* play the inner game.

If you are actively engaged in sport, you should now be able to see how best to use visualization to help you achieve success. Remember that the golden rule is to *visualize* the result that you want to achieve. Visualization does not replace good technique or experience or the necessary skills, but it enables the unconscious to play a full part in ensuring desired results.

for the dive, the ballet dancer waiting for her cue to go on stage for an exacting solo is visualizing her steps, the ski jumper waiting at the top of the ramp is mentally rehearsing what he is about to do, and visualizing the perfect landing.

Visualization and the Martial Arts

Some of the best instances of the power of visualization in sport come from the martial arts – judo, T'ai Chi, Karate, archery, Kendo etc. Though they can be used for self-defence, the true purpose of the martial arts is the development of the precise one-pointed concentration known as *mindfulness* (in which the mind is free of distractions and focused solely on the moment), together with the effective use of the subtle non-physical energies referred to as *chi* in China and as *ki* in Japan, and above all, of the realization of one's own true nature. The martial arts are in fact more truly described as meditative spiritual exercises than as sport. A whole philosophy, intricate yet simple, lies behind them, and they are never approached lightly by serious practitioners who revere them as a key to the deeper mysteries of life itself. There are many books on the martial arts, some good, others less so, but one of the best introductions is a slim volume by Eugen Herrigel, *Zen in the Art of Archery*, the success of which is demonstrated by the fact that from its first appearance in a beautiful English translation by R F C Hull in 1953 it has never been out of print. Further proof of its influence comes from the number of attempts to copy the formula in later years by the proliferation of books with titles that start with the words *Zen in the Art of …* (and follow them with oddities such as *Social Work* or *Coarse Fishing*).

Herrigel was a German professor of philosophy who spent six years lecturing in Japan, and who took up archery as a path to an understanding of Zen Buddhism. Herrigel found a remarkable teacher in the Zen master Kenzo Awa, who patiently but firmly (Herrigel had a great deal of Western mental baggage to unlearn) initiated him into archery. The archer, Kenzo Awa insisted to Herrigel, must become one with his target if his arrow is to find it. The ego, the conscious mind, must be set aside, while the archer – in the Japanese style – takes hold of the bow in total concentration, raises it above his head, pulls back the bow string, then lowers the bow to the correct position and releases the arrow without the slightest jerk of the hand. Only if this jerk is absent – despite the enormous tension of the bow string – is the archer free of ego and with his mind at one with the target. Thus he has to allow himself to stand, as Kenzo Awo puts it, 'egoless at the point of highest tension', a quality of mind and body that then becomes effortlessly present when faced by the tensions of life itself.

The point is that the archer, the arrow and the target become one, and without any interference from the ego (i.e. from the sense that '*I* am doing this action') the archer allows 'it', the subliminal energy of ki, to loose the string and send the arrow flying straight and true towards the target. Ultimately, the archer is in fact aiming at himself, because there is no distinction between himself and the target. All this is difficult to understand without some knowledge of Zen (or without reading the book), but even a brief summary such as this helps demonstrate how we can use the power of the unconscious mind over the actions of the body. When Herrigel is going through a particularly difficult stage, in which it appears as if he will never be able to allow the arrow to fly from the bow as effortlessly, in Kenzo Awa's words, as 'snow sliding from a leaf', Kenzo Awa tells Herrigel that his difficulty is that he has 'a too wilful will', and thinks that if he does not perform the action of loosing the arrow himself 'it does not happen'. Kenzo Awa constantly tells him that once the 'wilful will' gets out of the way, 'it' – the unconscious, the inner power of chi or ki, the spirit, call it what you will – is able to bring about the desired result.

You will note the similarities between the modern concept of the inner game and Kenzo Awa's teachings that arise from the centuries-old tradition of the martial arts. In addition, we have ample evidence of the extraordinary abilities to direct and use the inner power of chi (ki) shown by those who master the physical contact forms of these arts such as Aikido and T'ai Chi. Whether this power is directed at an opponent, or used internally to render certain parts of the body impervious to injury, the master practitioner is able to perform extraordinary feats of strength, so much so that a seemingly frail elderly man is able to throw younger and much heavier men across the room (see for example Payne 1981, Horwitz, T, Kimmelman, S, and Lui, H H 1982, and Koichi, T 1982). Such things are not a matter of belief but of objective observation.

The philosophy behind the martial arts goes back more than 2,000 years, and remains an integral part of Eastern psycho-spiritual traditions – not only of Zen Buddhism but of Taoism and Hinduism. This philosophy, based not upon superstition but upon an innate conception of the true nature of reality, has it that instead of being made up of individual objects (animal, vegetable and mineral), the underlying reality behind all things is that of unity. And not only are the elements that compose the material world identical within all things, consciousness itself is an expression of a similar unity. Individual minds are not separate from each other, and not localized within our heads as we assume, nor are they separate from the energies that manifest as the outer world. Far from being speculative, such a philosophy is supported at a number of points by some of the concepts arising from modern findings in quantum physics (the physics that studies the mysteries within the atom), in particular the concepts of unity, of the non-local nature of mind, and of the interaction between mind and the physical world.

If we now go back to Herrigel and his experiences with Zen archery, we see that the idea of a connection between the mind (or spirit), the arrow and the target is not at all fanciful. At the level of ultimate reality they are indeed one, and by allowing the mind to realize this oneness at the moment the arrow is released, the chances (we might say ultimately the inevitability) of hitting the target becomes a reality. On one occasion Kenzo Awa demonstrates this to Herrigel by taking him into the archery hall at night, when the hall is lit only by a single taper placed above the target. Kenzo Awa looses two arrows towards the invisible target, and when the lights are turned on Herrigel sees that not only have they both hit the bull, the accuracy is so great that the second arrow has precisely split the first one.

Most sportsmen and women develop their own methods of visualization, but in all cases the intention is the same, to unite two objects together. Whether those two objects are a golf ball and the flag, the arrow and the target, the high jumper and the clear space above the bar, the sprinter and the finishing line, the mind aims to bridge the distance between them, so that effectively they become one. The player *sees* himself achieving the goal, and the stronger he is able to do so, the better the chances of success. It would be unrealistic to suppose that visualization alone will ensure success. Visualization is simply the final stage in the journey towards the goal, not the only stage. But for most successful players it is an indispensable stage, and if anything happens to interrupt it they will, if at all possible, go back to the beginning and start the visualization all over again. Only when they are satisfied with it will they strike the ball, release the shot or begin the run-up to the high jump bar.

Box 6: What Shoots?

After five years of diligent practice Herrigel is at last able to loose the arrow without ego. Kenzo Awa asks him, 'Do you now understand what I mean by "It shoots"?'

Herrigel answers, 'I'm afraid I don't understand anything any more … Is it "I" who draws the bow or is it the bow that draws me? … Do I hit the goal or does the goal hit me? … Bow, arrow and ego all melt into one another so that I can no longer separate them … even the need to separate them has gone. For as soon as I take the bow and shoot, everything becomes so clear and straightforward and so ridiculously simple.'

'Now at last,' the master answers, 'the bow string has cut right through you.'

When Herrigel leaves Japan after his six-year stay the master tells him, 'You have become a different person in the course of these years. For this is what the art of archery means: a profound and far-reaching contest of the archer with himself … You will see with other eyes and measure with other measures.'

The master tells Herrigel never to write to him 'but send me photographs from time to time so that I can see how you draw the bow. Then I shall know everything I need to know.' Finally in parting he gives Herrigel his best bow and tells him, 'Give it not into the hands of the curious! And when you have passed beyond it do not lay it up in remembrance! Destroy it so that nothing remains but a heap of ashes.'

(When the man without ego departs this life he leaves nothing negative behind, and has no reason to return.)

Chapter 4

Visualization for Health and Healing

All Healing is Ultimately Self-Healing

Visualization exercises have become increasingly popular in the area of health and healing, having received a particular impetus from the publication in 1978 of *Getting Well Again* by Simonton, Matthews-Simonton and Creighton. Written by medical doctors, the authors put forward evidence that visualization can sometimes help produce healing even in the case of serious physical illness. Visualization enlists the support of the unconscious, which is then instrumental in mustering the body's healing mechanisms. It is important to remember that all healing is ultimately self-healing. The treatment provided by doctors, whether medical or surgical, facilitates this self-healing but does not in itself produce it. Even antibiotics, which destroy invading bacteria, do not actually heal the sickness the bacteria have caused. Only the body can do that, and it does so of course at an unconscious level. Indeed, the majority of the body's activity takes place at this level. The central nervous system is involved in consciousness and in the intentional physical activity such as movement to which consciousness gives rise, whereas the autonomic nervous system is involved at the unconscious level in all our myriad other physical functions such as heartbeat, blood circulation and oxygenation, digestion, cellular activity, and of course healing. For many years Western science believed that the central nervous system and the autonomic nervous system were so independent of each other that the conscious mind could have no influence upon what went on in the autonomic system, but more recent research shows that consciousness can in fact get messages through to it. This does not mean that the mind consciously manipulates the autonomic physical processes. These still take place at an unconscious level. What it does mean is that by entering the proper mindset – and in particular through the use of visualization – the conscious mind can convey its wishes to the unconscious, which then takes over the task of trying to carry them out.

This being the case it follows that, although not intending to do so, the mind can also produce harmful effects in the body. Estimates vary, but as we said earlier it seems likely that one-third or more of all physical illnesses have their origins in the mind. Without our realizing it, our frame of mind, our emotions, our feelings and of course the way we 'see' ourselves all have direct effects upon the body. A simple example is that of extreme anxiety or anger which can temporarily raise the blood pressure by as much as 50 per cent above its normal resting level as the body gears itself up for fight or flight. Another example is the way in which stress can interfere with appetite, with sleep, with digestion, with heart rate and with breathing. At more extreme levels, intense emotion can even trigger heart attacks or strokes in those who are at risk of these conditions. Serious long-standing conditions can also be the result of states of mind and of emotion, and prolonged stress may affect the immune system, rendering us more likely to succumb to infections and possibly to a wide range of other conditions.

Any of the usual forms of meditation can assist the body by relaxing tensions and calming the mind. And once the mind becomes quiet and peaceful so does the body. If the body is quiet and peaceful it is much better able to allow the autonomic processes within it to carry out their task of maintaining health.

A simple but important example can show us how visualization, used as part of a meditation programme, can be particularly effective in assisting these processes. Whenever we have anything wrong with us physically, we all too quickly incorporate the problem into the way we 'see' ourselves. Let us suppose we have a bad back. Once the trouble persists for more than a few days, we begin to think of ourselves as someone who 'has' a bad back. We fall into the habit of moving as if we have a bad back even though this usually means we tense our muscles even more and thus make things worse. We get into the habit of expecting sympathy from others, and of sitting or lying down whenever we have the chance. In no time at all we really are a person who 'has' – we could even say 'is' – a bad back.

This arises from doing all the wrong things. Certainly the trouble has to be checked medically in case there is structural damage to the spine (in the great majority of cases there isn't), but equally importantly we have to drop the idea that we 'have' a bad back. What in fact we have is a very good back that has carried us through life ever since we learnt as a small child to stand upright, a back that has endured all kind of misuse such as bad posture, bad sitting positions, unnecessary tensions, lack of exercise, and the tendency to take part in sport or to lift heavy weights without the necessary preparation. We also have a back that, provided there is no structural damage to the spine, will quickly right itself given the chance. Which is where visualization comes in. If we *think* of ourselves as moving stiffly and painfully, this sends the message to the unconscious that we are stuck with our disability. One of the worst things we can do for non-structural back pain is to immobilize ourselves. We should move as much as possible, and aim to keep the muscles of the back relaxed rather than stiff with tension. We should start by visualizing ourselves moving freely again, perhaps running along the beach or through fields and experiencing the pleasure of pain-free movement. This is not a prelude to translating the visualization into immediate reality. We have to take things slowly and sensibly. But we are sending the message to the unconscious that free, unhindered movement is the natural way of being, and that we intend to get back to this way of being as quickly as possible. The result is that the unconscious understands our intention and energizes the healing process to accomplish it.

Visualization can also aid the development of good posture that helps avoid back, joint and muscle problems in the first place. If the Good Lord were to redesign the human body, now that we walk upright as a species, he would probably put the spine along the centre of the body rather than along the back. If it were in the centre, like the tent pole in a round bell tent, the weight of the upper body would be much more evenly distributed and it would be under a great deal less strain. However, as things are, the spine is at the back, which means that if we slump forward it bears all the weight of the abdomen and the torso, like a sapling bent by the wind. Watch most people, at any age from adolescence onwards, and you will see what I mean. Little wonder that as the years go by the spine begins to protest. In Chapter 2 we touched on this when we carried out visualizations into how we look and how we move, but there is much more that can be done, as we can see if we study T'ai Chi, one of the most profound of the martial arts. A fundamental visualization used in T'ai Chi is to imagine that there is a thread connecting the crown of the head to the sky, effort-lessly holding the spine upright like a stack of coins. This visualization not only corrects the posture, but gives the body a feeling of lightness, as if the sky as well as the earth is responsible for our ability to walk on two legs. The Alexander Technique (see Box 7), an excellent set of teachings for re-educating the mind and body, suggests a variant of this, namely that we should simply 'think up'. Whenever we 'think up', the body automatically responds and straightens itself in response to an inner picture of what 'thinking up' means for our posture. By practising the visu-alization of the connecting thread or 'thinking up', the unconscious will quickly get the message and the body will respond accordingly.

Box 7: The Alexander Technique and Other Ways of Self-Healing

The concept of self-healing goes back many centuries, but in more recent times there are certain writers who stand out, not only for keeping the concept alive, but for adding new ideas to it and demonstrating the value of these ideas by healing themselves and others. One good example is the French 19th-/early 20th-century pharmacist Émile Coué who discovered the power of positive thinking, which involves telling oneself that one *is* as one wants to be. Coué's influence upon later practitioners has been considerable, and the best known of the instructions he recommends that one should give oneself, namely, 'Day by day I am getting better and better', (repeated regularly every day) has passed into the literature of self-healing.

Another good example is Matthias Alexander, a contemporary of Coué, who published one of his most influential books in 1932 (*The Use of the Self*). His work was applauded by luminaries such as the distinguished writer Aldous Huxley and the educationalist Professor John Dewey. Alexander developed a set of practices, known as the Alexander Technique, that continue to gain in popularity to this day. The Alexander Technique focuses on re-educating our use of the body, and shows how this re-education can be effective in healing a number of physical and psychological conditions that at first sight would not appear to be connected with actions such as how we stand and how we sit. Visualizing our bodies sitting, standing and moving properly (as detailed in Chapter 2) are a major help in this re-education. Wilfred Barlow, a friend and collaborator of Alexander, wrote what remains one of the best introductions to his work (Barlow 1979).

Further landmarks in self-healing, this time with an emphasis primarily upon the use of visualization, include the publication some years ago of two books by a retired senior naval officer, Admiral E H Shattock. Shattock demonstrated that one does not necessarily need to have a medical or psychological background in order to develop successful visualization methods (Shattock 1979 and 1982).

The effectiveness of methods such as those of Coué and Alexander can be greatly enhanced if they are accompanied by visualizations. Some idea of the wide use of visualization, and of other ways of using the mind to heal the body, is covered in three excellent books by Goleman and Guerin (1993), Moyers (1993), and Benson (1996).

Healing Energy

Using visualization to help maintain good posture also assists with joint and muscle problems elsewhere in the body, particularly those in the neck and shoulders. Less well known is the fact that it also benefits digestion (slumping after a heavy meal is one of the worst things we can do to the stomach) and helps prevent a middle-aged spread. Health is the natural condition of the body, and given the right conditions, health is what the body is trying to restore. However, if the health problem has to do with internal organs rather than with the joints or muscles, visualization is used in a rather different way. It is here that the work of the Simontons, referred to at the start of the chapter, and of others using similar methods is particularly relevant. Fundamentally, visualization is now used to imagine healing energy being drawn into the body with each breath and flowing on the out-breath to the parts that require healing. In past years the sceptical Western mind has been quick to reject the idea that anything called 'healing energy' can be accessed by the breathing, particularly when claims have been made that this energy can be drawn into the body not only through the nose and mouth but – although still linked to the breath – through one or other of the so-called *chakras*. In Eastern psycho-spiritual traditions and yoga, the chakras are subliminal energy centres, said to occupy seven positions in the body ranging upwards from the perineum to the crown of the head, and are considered to be centres of the subtle energy that sustains the body and maintains physical mental and spiritual health. At best, Western sceptics are prepared only to accept that if visualization of healing energy does help produce results it is a consequence merely of the placebo effect (the benefits people derive from simply *believing* that something is doing them good) rather than of anything that really exists.

However, the indisputable fact is that visualizations of healing energy flowing through the body can help produce results. Known as *prana* in yogic philosophy and probably analogous to the subtle chi (or ki) energy mentioned in the last chapter (and also perhaps to the *élan vital* described by the great French philosopher Henri Bergson and the *orgone energy* or *bioenergy* claimed actually to be observed by the Austrian psychoanalyst Wilhelm Reich and others), this healing energy – or life force energy – is said to pervade the cosmos and to constitute the vital spark that is the essence of physical life itself. It is said to be drawn into the body, together with air, on every breath, and that the relevant visualization practices, known as *prana visualization,* can enable it to deliver full potency to the body and to be directed to those parts most in need of it.

Prana visualization can be done in the normal meditation position, or lying outstretched on the floor provided one does not drift off into sleep. If you choose the latter position lie flat on your back with arms beside you and the legs out straight. The eyes can be open or closed. If you can do so without strain, keep the lower back against the floor so that the spine is well aligned as in sitting meditation. Breathe normally a few times in order to relax, taking care to draw the air first into the abdomen then into the lower chest and finally into the upper chest (the so-called *complete yogic breath*). Do not put too much effort into this or try to fill the lungs to bursting point. The aim is not to over-breathe, which can be dangerous, but to breathe properly, using the appropriate capacity of the lungs but slowing the breathing down at the same time so that in total you are actually taking in no more air than usual.

Concentrate on the threefold rhythm of breathing deep within the body – lower abdomen, lower chest, upper chest. Pay careful attention to the breath. Notice that this threefold rhythm starts with the abdomen – more specifically with the diaphragm, the largest muscle in the body – and that it seems as if the breath is entering at this point and then flowing upwards until it reaches the upper chest. Because it is in harmony with the way the breath seems to be moving, prana visualization is easier to do (and has a profounder feel to it) if you imagine the breath starting from the abdomen rather than entering at the nose and flowing downwards.

Follow the threefold, upward rhythm of the breathing until the body is fully relaxed and the rhythm takes over your full awareness. Now visualize the breath as white life-giving energy that suffuses the body with vigour, renewal and healing. Continue to regard the breath as starting at the abdomen, but when the visualization is fully established – and certainly when you are more experienced – you can change to imagining it entering the body at the so-called base chakra, situated at the perineum (the area just behind the genitals), or at the very lowest point in the body, namely the heels. *Heel breathing* and *chakra breathing*, as they are called, are not as difficult as they may sound. Heel breathing has the advantage of seeming to infuse the whole body with energy at each breath, while chakra breathing involves visualizing this energy rising from the base chakra upwards through each chakra in turn and ending at the crown of the head. If and when you decide to use either of these methods, place your awareness at the heels, or at the base chakra, and visualize the cool air drawn in with the breath at the point concerned. Both these methods have been used in yoga for many centuries, and the degree of control over the physical body that yogis are able to gain with breathing and visualization meditations has been demonstrated scientifically on many occasions (see for example Goleman and Gurin 1993). When using chakra breathing or heel breathing, the threefold rhythm is now replaced by a single smooth upward flow of the breath passing in turn through each of the seven chakras (situated respectively at the perineum, at a point four inches below the navel, at the navel itself, at the heart, at the throat, at a point between and just above the eyes, and at the crown of the head).

Whichever of these three methods of pranic breathing you use, the out-breath is visualized as sending the energy, still in the form of white light, throughout the rest of the body, and in particular to any points that require healing. Many people report that the sense of coolness they felt at the heels or at the base chakra with each in-breath now floods the body, bringing with it not only healing but a sense of great tenderness and acceptance towards the self. As the symbolic colour of this energy is white, it also brings with it a feeling of cleansing and of purification. Its source is said, in yoga, to be the source from which all creation and all life arose in the immeasurable past and from which all creation and all life arises to this day. It is the elixir upon which we depend for our very existence, and that flows through every cell in the body.

Many people report that the body begins to feel light, as if it could float away, while others report a vibrating, tingling feeling, as if the body is being washed clean. Now complete this part of the meditation by visualizing the energy, as you breath out, flowing down the arms and out at the fingertips. The whole body is now illuminated with this visualized white light, with each part participating in the flow of this cleansing energy.

What is Actually Happening?

At this point people sometimes want to return to the question of what is really taking place. Is this talk of energy, and white light, pure imagination or is something objective actually happening? We know from research with scientific instruments that the so-called *meridians*, the subtle energy channels said to run throughout the body and into which needles are inserted during acupuncture to balance energies and assist healing, do actually register minute changes in electrical conductivity on the surface of the skin. Although more work needs to be done, this supports the idea that there are objective energy systems in the body, unrecognized by biologists. Furthermore, acupuncture works, particularly in the management of pain, and we have good reason to suppose that the subtle energy involved in prana visualization, although facilitated and directed by imagination, operates at an objective level. In the West we tend always to think in terms of 'either/or'. In this case 'either' prana visualization is imagination 'or' it is real. But much of life experience cannot be reduced to these opposites. Eastern thought has always accepted that sometimes 'both/and' is more appropriate than 'either/or'. In terms of 'both/and', prana visualization is 'both' imagination 'and' reality. The two things are not alternatives, and if used, as described above, they bring together two different planes of reality.

We can go further still, and point to the close relationship between imagination and objective reality shown by recent research using a brain monitoring technique called *Positron Emission Tomography* (better known these days by its initials, PET). PET scans of the brain reveal that whether people are imagining something or actually experiencing it, the same parts of the cerebral cortex are activated. Thus, the optical cortex is activated when the individual is engaged in visualization, the auditory cortex when music is being imagined, and the sensory cortex when the imagination conjures up the sense of touch. And, just as when things are actually seen, heard or touched, the imagination transmits signals to the lower brain centres (whose activity is largely unconscious) and from there they are transmitted to the autonomic nervous system that produces physical responses. Not only do these results show that imagination can have effects upon the body that are similar to those produced by direct experience, they also appear to show that the more vivid and intense the imaginative experience, the more real it seems to the brain, and the stronger and more extensive are the signals sent to the unconscious and to the body. Therefore, by imagining an experience – in the present case the flow of subtle energy through the body – we render the body more receptive to the actual receipt of this energy. Real experience literally follows imagined experience. Through imagination the mind activates the appropriate centres in the brain, and the rest follows from there.

In the area of visualization and meditation, it is therefore important not to allow scepticism, based purely upon limited theories of reality, to deny oneself the opportunity to benefit from centuries-old practices that can readily be put to the test of direct experience. And, just as the open, receptive mind can through imagination facilitate the action of subtle energies, so the sceptical mind can inhibit this action, rather as a tap that has been turned off does not allow water to flow (and if our undue scepticism turns off the tap we have only ourselves to blame for going thirsty).

Prana Visualization for Specific Problems

We return to this issue in due course below, but before we do so there is a further part to prana visualization. The practices described so far allow the whole body to benefit from the prana energy, but suppose we have a particular problem in one area of it? In that case, prana visualization traditions teach that the energy can be directed by visualization to flow to the area concerned. In order to do this, on the out-breath the practitioner visualizes the white light that symbolizes this energy streaming towards the affected part, as if propelled by the breath itself, and bathing it with healing, soothing power. Once again, with a little practice, this visualization can become firmly established. If desired, visualization can be accompanied on each out-breath with words of one's own choosing, said silently or out loud, such as 'healing energy' or 'healing light'.

There is a further variant that many people find valuable, particularly if they are going through a period of stress or, for personal reasons, feel in need of a purification ritual. The basics are the same except that this time, on the in-breath, one imagines the white light flushing out all the stresses and strains as it flows upwards through the body, then discarding them on the out-breath as a grey (or even a black) cloud. The meditation is continued until the dark cloud becomes progressively lighter on each out-breath, and is completed when it retains its initial purity, suggesting that the body has been cleansed. No attempt should be made to rush this colour change. Usually it happens of its own accord, and one simply watches the process, but some people report that, as they begin to feel more relaxed and more at ease with themselves, they are gradually aware of changing the colour consciously.

The Simontons, mentioned at the start of this chapter, developed another interesting variant to the above practices and found it to be associated with a range of medical benefits such as: pain and anxiety relief; increased ability to cope with disease; improved capacity to prepare for and recover from surgery; and a greater tolerance of the side effects of medication. However – and this applies to *all* the practices described in this book – they stress that their visualization method is to be used alongside, and not instead of, orthodox medical treatments, and point out that visualization does not run the risk, as do some other unorthodox therapies, of interfering in any way with the effectiveness of these treatments. Working initially with cancer sufferers, the Simontons taught their patients to visualize the cells of their immune systems fighting and destroying the cancer cells. This method is obviously more appropriate to conditions where the body is under attack than to matters of more general health, although, even when the body is under attack, the Simonton method makes it clear that one can use whatever images one prefers. These may consist of the army of the immune system attacking and defeating an invading army, or a form of prana visualizations in which the patient pictures the healing white light washing away and disposing of whatever is invading it. The emphasis is always upon a relaxed and open frame of mind, and as vivid and effective a series of visualizations as possible.

All visualization practices possess the added advantage of helping patients become more in touch with their feelings about their illness. In the case of illnesses such as asthma, arthritis and certain skin problems, which may have a strong link to emotional states, visualization meditations may help identify these states and assist the process of dealing with them. For example, if one is using prana meditation one can ask the white light to identify an image or a symbol that represents the states concerned. Since illnesses such as the ones just mentioned appear to involve the immune system turning against itself, often this image or symbol may turn out to be a self-destructive one. For example, it may be a stern, disapproving, punitive figure that is always finding fault with one and invoking feelings of guilt and self-rejection. Once identified, the meditator can then decide how best to cope with this figure. To the surprise of some, frequently the best approach is not one of confrontation. Instead, it is recognized that the disapproving figure is actually trying, however misguidedly, to be helpful – in other words to make the sufferer a better person. The response then becomes one of thanks for their efforts, and explaining to them that they have been too extreme in their methods, which have in fact become counterproductive. Instead of helping to create a better person, they have been hindering the processes of positive self-development. Following the acceptance of this by the figure, a

dialogue can then ensue on how he or she can help in more productive ways. If none can be found, then the figure can be
encouraged to take a rest from their self-imposed task, and
be peaceful and relaxed from now on. This dialogue may need to
be acted out several times, but no part of the mind or of the emotions really wants to spend time fighting another part. The natural
state of the mind is one of harmony with itself. This is the state of
mind with which we are born, and it is only our life experience that
upsets things. The fundamental purpose of a visualization meditation involving a dialogue with oneself – as in fact with all
visualization meditations – is to restore things to this natural state.

The meditation can be taken further, if required, by asking the
white light to find an 'inner adviser' or helper who is there to guide
and support. Dialogues can also then be allowed to develop
between this adviser and the guilt-provoking and more punitive
part of oneself.

Visualization for Self-Defence

We can now return to the question of whether we are open or not
to unseen spiritual (from beings in other dimensions of reality) and
psychic (from beings in this world) influences from outside
ourselves. The esoteric traditions of the West, together with the
psycho-spiritual traditions of the East, have always been in no
doubt that we are, and equally in no doubt that these influences
can be negative as well as positive. Western science regards this
idea as fanciful, but, as we have already implied, Western science
has no monopoly of the truth, particularly when it comes to
matters of the spirit and of the powers of the mind, and no
scientist who has studied the evidence yielded by human
experience would claim that it has. One of the most obvious
examples of external influences is the ability of the human mind,
under certain conditions, sometimes to influence directly the
minds of others by what traditionally is known as telepathy.
The evidence for this ability, based not only upon the personal

experience of countless people over the centuries but also upon carefully controlled laboratory experiments, is now so strong that it is no longer open to serious doubt (see Radin 1997 for a full survey). And, if someone else can influence your mind by their thoughts, whether consciously or unconsciously, can they also influence your body? The first serious attempt to answer this question was by Professor William Braud, then at the Mind Science Foundation in San Antonio, Texas. Braud's ingenious experiment was to see if red blood cells could be protected by human thought from swelling and bursting (an effect known as *haemolysis*) when placed in test tubes containing a weak saline solution. The people supplying the thought consisted of 32 technicians with no training in work of this kind and, thus, with no proven skills to help them in their attempts.

The 32 individuals were shown colour slides of healthy blood cells, and asked to visualize them remaining healthy when put into the solution. Ten test tubes were used, and samples of blood were also put into a further ten test tubes that were used as controls and not subjected to visualization. The individuals were placed in a different room from the test tubes, and the rate of haemolysis was accurately measured photometrically, i.e. by passing a light beam through the solution. Results showed that the blood cells subjected to visualization disintegrated significantly less quickly than those in the control test tubes. In fact, so great was the difference between what occurred in the experimental test tubes and what occurred in the control test tubes that it would only be expected to happen by chance alone 1 in 5,000 times (Braud 1990).

The red blood cells were not actually in the human body when the experiment took place, but this experiment, conducted by an eminent and very highly regarded scientist, is of great importance, and should have achieved far more scientific and public attention than it has done. It demonstrates, beyond any reasonable doubt, that human thought, even at a distance and even when used by individuals with no special training, through visualization can actually influence (in this case by protecting) living human blood cells.

Research of a similar kind, now known as *Direct Mental Interaction with Living Systems* (DMILS for short), is currently being conducted in a number of scientific centres. The procedure usually employed differs from that used by William Braud in that the subjects of the experiments are actually living people. Subjects work in pairs, one as a 'sender' and the other as a 'receiver' who is monitored for electrodermal reaction (the slight dampening of the skin at moments of emotional arousal or tension), during the experiment. The two people are isolated from each other, and the sender is asked to visualize the receiver in either a calming situation (e.g. relaxing on a beach) or in an arousing situation (either exciting or alarming). The whole experiment lasts some 20 minutes, and during this time the sender is instructed by computer at 30-second intervals either to visualize a calming or an arousing situation.

Results from numerous experiments show that the sender's electrodermal reaction turns out to be significantly more marked when the sender is visualizing an arousing situation than when he or she is visualizing a calming one (Schmidt, Schneider, Utts, J, and Wallach 2002). Moreover, these results are apparent even when the receiver is not consciously aware that any emotional change has taken place in his or her body. In other words, the visualization seems to have an effect upon the receiver at an unconscious level. This is an enormously important finding. Not only is the body of one individual influenced by the visualizations carried out by another, but the first individual is not even aware of what is happening.

This raises the further possibility that influences of this kind may occur even when the individual carrying out the visualization has no intention of affecting the other person, for example when one person is simply picturing another enjoying themselves or in an awkward situation such as a stressful interview or a missed flight connection. If nothing else, this possibility is a good reason for trying always to think well of people when we picture them in the mind's eye. In medieval times, when both blessing and cursing were believed to be an effective way of benefiting or harming people at a distance, our medieval ancestors would doubtless have strongly endorsed this advice.

Do We Know if Others are Staring at Us?

On the strength of other recent research, it seems that not only visualizing images but actually looking at them can have a direct mental influence upon what is seen, at least if the subject concerned is another person. Many men and women believe that they can cause others to look around simply by staring at them from behind, and that they also know when they are being stared at in turn. This seems like another fanciful idea. Sceptics will argue that we are simply unaware of many occasions when we are being stared at, and that although we may *remember* the times when by chance someone looked around while we were staring at them, we *forget* the other times when staring had no effect at all. However, it is easy enough to put the so-called staring phenomenon to experimental test. We can separate two people in the laboratory by a device known as a one-way mirror, an ingenious piece of equipment that serves as a mirror on one side and as a window on the other, with the result that the person on the mirror side cannot see the person on the window side, although the latter has a good view of the former. We can then set up a computer that emits a series of signals at intervals, half of which instruct the person on the window side to stare at the person on the mirror side, and half of which instruct him to look away. The person on the mirror side hears a beep on each of these signals, and has to guess if it means staring is taking place or not.

We would expect that by chance alone half of these guesses would be correct on average and half incorrect, yet the experiments show that some people really do know when they are being stared at. The results, however, seem to be influenced by the attitude of mind of the experimenter supervising the tests – sceptical investigators get chance results, open-minded ones get positive results, supporting the idea mentioned earlier that sceptics inhibit psychic performance in some way. Professor William Braud, whose work on visualization and the protection of red blood cells was described earlier, even reports that the staring phenomenon happens when individuals stare at a closed-circuit television image of someone seated in a distant room rather than at the person themselves. Instead of asking his subjects to say when they were being stared at, Professor Braud monitored their electrodermal activity, and found it differed significantly during the periods in which staring was taking place, even though they were not aware at which times this was happening (Braud, Schafer, and Andrews 1990). As in the DMILS studies described earlier, this suggests we are subject to unseen influences from others even when we are unaware of the fact. Braud's results were confirmed in a similar study by Dr Marilyn Schlitz, who in a further experiment demonstrated the significant difference in results obtained in work of this kind by open-minded experimenters, such as herself, and sceptical experimenters such as Professor Richard Wiseman (Wiseman and Schlitz 1997).

Psychic Attack?

These studies lend some credence to the old idea that one can be under 'psychic attack' from another person or group of people. People who claim to be victims of such an 'attack' report suffering mysterious physical malaise and psychological problems such as panic and nightmares. We have no hard evidence on whether these disabilities are imaginary or real, but it would be interesting to assess if the subjects in DMILS and in staring experiments are able to 'protect' themselves against the unseen influence of others, and demonstrate this by showing a difference in electrodermal response between the sessions when they are 'protecting' themselves and those when they are not.

What form might these attempts at 'protection' take? Much guidance on psychic attacks is given in the esoteric literature, all of which centres upon the use of the powers of visualization. Most frequently quoted is the practice of imagining oneself surrounded by a cocoon of white light. Linked to prana visualizations, this involves breathing in white light and then, on the out-breath, visualizing it leaving the body through the arms, feet and the crown of the head and forming into the white cocoon. With each breath the cocoon becomes clearer and stronger, and it is visualized as remaining intact even when the meditation is concluded. From time to time during the day – and particularly at night before going to sleep – the attention is returned to the cocoon to check that the visualization is still clear and strong. If it should be less clear, then it is reinforced by returning briefly to the breathing exercise.

If nothing else, the experience gained in carrying out this procedure certainly helps to further develop the powers of visualization. At a psychological level the procedure also enhances self-confidence and self-awareness. As with prana visualization, it is up to the individual to decide whether any other positive results (such as feeling stronger physically and more tranquil mentally and emotionally) are owing to the power of the mind over the body or to some objective use of unseen forces. One thing is clear. It is unlikely the procedure will be of any use if one decides in advance that it isn't going to work. The comparative effect on results in psychical research of scepticism on the one hand, and belief or open-mindedness on the other, is in fact one of the most consistent findings to emerge from laboratory experiments over the years. Often referred to as the sheep (believers) and goats (non-believers) effect, it was first documented by leading researcher Dr Gertrude Schmeidler as far back as the 1940s and indicates that if we want positive results in any area of psychical research, whether as experimenters or when working on ourselves, we are far more likely to obtain them if we have an open-minded approach than a rigidly sceptical one. Mediums also insist that they find it harder to get spirit communications for those who disbelieve in them than for those who accept they may occur. If someone begins a session with a medium with a rigidly sceptical attitude, then he or she will normally get what they expect, i.e. nothing. Most mediums insist that they have nothing against unprejudiced scepticism, the scepticism that is prepared to judge on results rather than on preconceptions – what they find inhibiting is the closed mind.

Some people consider that surrounding themselves with a visualized cocoon of white light helps them to avoid picking up colds and flu while in public places at times when infections are likely. We have no experimental scientific evidence to back up or to dismiss this claim because in psychical research we are dealing with phenomena that do not obey the laws of known physical science, and that cannot always be demonstrated under experimental conditions. And science very much dislikes accepting the reality of anything when it has no acceptable theory to explain how it happens. However, it is well to remember that even in science this reliance upon theories does not always hold good. For example, although in physics we talk about magnetic 'fields', the truth is that we still cannot explain what these 'fields' actually are. We know they occur, and that they occur consistently and predictably, but as to their real nature we are still in the dark. Even the term magnetic 'field' is only a convenient label for the area within which the magnetic effect operates. Thus, the fact that we do not know what the psychic 'effect' actually is – whether produced by visualizations, telepathy, clairvoyance or perhaps even by a mysterious force called prana – should not in itself be a reason for automatically assuming that it therefore does not exist. True, it works neither consistently nor predictably, but then neither do other effects associated with human behaviour such as genius or love. Elusive and following no known laws, sometimes these effects occur and sometimes they do not, and in spite of many years of research we still cannot be more precise than that.

One of the very many exciting things about the psychic effect is that, unlike so many other forms of experimental scientific investigation that require sophisticated and expensive equipment and specialist knowledge, most areas of it require nothing more from the investigator than the necessary background knowledge and the activity of his or her own mind. Thus, the best advice for those interested in using the kind of visualizations detailed in this chapter is to adopt an open enquiring mind, give to the work the necessary time and patience, and then observe the results. Only by doing so can one judge their value.

Does the Aura Exist?

Visualizing oneself surrounded by a cocoon of white light touches on the concept of the so-called aura, a concept that has been with us since ancient times. As the aura is supposed to be actually seen rather than just visualized, extended discussion of it lies outside this book. However, judging by their art and their writings, the early Egyptians, Greeks and Romans all appear to have believed in the aura, so the subject needs a mention, particularly as the 16th-century scholar Paracelsus, regarded by some as one of the founders of modern medicine, considered it to exist, as did the great 18th-century Swedish scientist and seer, Emmanuel Swedenborg, who wrote in his *Spiritual Diary* of a 'spiritual sphere surrounding every one, as well as a natural and corporeal one'.

The aura is said to be a cocoon of vital energy that surrounds the human body, closely following its shape and extending outwards some three or four inches. There are various explanations for its existence, but common to most of them is the belief that it is the outer limit of the subtle energy system that contains the energy meridians permeating the body and that sustains physical life. Auras are said to surround all living beings, including animals and plants, and are even considered by some to radiate from minerals. There is also a widespread belief, shared by many natural healing traditions, that the energy body, sometimes called the *etheric body* leaves the physical body together with the spiritual body at death, and disintegrates three days later leaving the spiritual body to continue its journey into the afterlife.

It is worth noting that a number of physicians and those associated with the medical profession have believed in this energy body. The 18th-century physician Anton Mesmer, the originator of mesmerism which later became associated, rightly or wrongly, with hypnotism, believed that it consisted of an electromagnetic force that could, in certain circumstances, be transmitted to others. The 19th-century German chemist Baron Karl von Reichenback referred to it as the *odic force,* and developed a number of experiments claimed to demonstrate its reality, one of which involved seating clairvoyants in darkened rooms and recording what they saw, which was reported to include flamelike energy radiating from the fingertips of humans, animals, plants and certain crystals. Said to contain the colours red, green, orange and violet, these flames appeared and disappeared, sometimes intermingled with sparks and with stars.

Dr Walter Kilner, the doctor in charge of what was then called electrotherapy at the prestigious St Thomas's Hospital in London, went further still and developed spectacles with lenses containing the coal tar dye dicyanin, which makes ultraviolet light visible, by means of which it was claimed the aura becomes visible. In the course of his experiments with these spectacles Kilner noted that, although male and female auras were the same in childhood, those of adult women tended to be more refined in texture than those of men. More importantly, he claimed to have discovered that the aura can be divided into three parts which he called respectively the etheric double (narrow and closest to the body), the inner aura (the most constant of the three) and the outer aura. In addition, he reported that auras appear to reveal the state of health of the individuals concerned. So consistent did this finding appear to be that in 1919 he developed a method said to diagnose illness based upon it (Kilner 1965). His death in 1920 brought this work to an end, and his theories have never been put to proper test.

This is not the case with *Kirlian Photography*, developed by Russian electrician Semyon Kirlian in 1939. The technique involves photographing objects placed in a high-voltage, high-frequency, low-amperage electric field. The results show a multicoloured corona around the image, thought by some actually to be the aura (sometimes renamed the biofield). Others consider it to be what Kilner called the etheric body. Critics reject these explanations, and claim the photographs merely show the discharge of electricity that occurs when an electrically grounded object emits sparks between itself and an electrode, generating an electrical field. Furthermore, they point out that similar photographs were reported as early as 1898 at a photographic exhibition, and that subsequent research in former Czechoslovakia, prior to Kirlian's work, found little of value in them. Another problem is that some of the findings that have attracted most attention have not been reliably replicated by other researchers – for example, a Kirlian photograph taken by Dr Thelma Moss (Moss 1979) during her research at the University of California's Center for Health Sciences showing that a severed section of leaf still appeared as a glowing outline on the edge of the leaf. However, questions still remain as to the exact cause of the Kirlian effect, and there are still those who consider it has a place in diagnostic medicine, and recommend that further properly funded research should be carried out.

Clairvoyants claim that they can see the aura without artificial aids, and attempts have been made to substantiate their claims. One simple test is for someone whose aura is said to be visible to go outside the room, leaving the door open. A signal, unseen by the clairvoyant, is then given to them to approach the open door, coming within two or three inches but without actually showing themselves. On an equal number of other occasions they are signalled to stay well back. On both approach and stay-back occasions the clairvoyant is asked say whether they can see the

Box 8: Scrying and the Psychomanteum

Scrying or crystal gazing has long been considered a form of clair-voyance, that is a method of gaining information about what is happening in distant places. Scrying is usually carried out with a crystal or glass ball (quartz is said to be better still) or even by gazing at the surface of a bowl of black ink. In a state of semi-trance the scryer is said to see images forming in the shiny surface in front of him, and at one time no serious student of the occult was without his crystal ball. However, with its association with fairground trickery, scrying fell into disrepute until recently, when largely through the work of Dr Raymond Moody (Moody and Perry 1994) it has resurfaced in the form of what is known as the *psychomanteum*.

The psychomanteum is basically a small darkened room in which the percipient sits in an upright chair with a low-wattage lamp on the floor behind him or her, and a mirror on the wall in front, situated just above eye level. After sitting in this way for a period of time, some people report seeing shadowy images in the mirror, typically of the deceased. Sometimes these images appear to take on a life of their own, and to speak and even seemingly to step out of the mirror and into the room. Dr Moody's research has shown that many bereaved people feel reassured of the reality of survival of death as a result of their experiences with the psychomanteum.

Since the images reported while in the psychomanteum or gazing into crystal balls are spontaneous, they are classed as visions rather than as visualizations. However, they share similarities with visualizations in that they appear to be produced by the unconscious. Given the right circumstances, whether these be dreams, the psychomanteum, or induced visualizations, the unconscious appears eager to take over and provide us with images of its own that may reveal not only deeper levels of our own being but other dimensions of spiritual reality.

aura or not. By chance alone he or she should get it right 50 per cent of times. If the score is significantly higher than this, and provided that care has been taken not to allow clues such as a shadow to give the game away, this provides some evidence that the aura has objective reality.

The test is not particularly scientific, but if it is properly conducted it can be quite useful. However, failure by the clairvoyant correctly to report the occasions when the aura is in theory visible does not necessarily mean that the latter does not exist. It is possible that auras are only visible when the body to which they belong is also on view. Thus, even though someone approaches the open door nothing is going to be seen if the body itself cannot be seen. As in so many areas connected with the paranormal, serious research is needed in order to establish once and for all whether there is anything in the concept of the aura or not. If auras, whatever their cause, do exist, and if they do give us reliable clues as to physical and perhaps even psychological health, then we should know more about them, and perhaps include them as part of the diagnostic armoury of orthodox medicine.

Chapter 5

Visualization and the Creative Mind

Creativity as Self-Exploration

We are all born with creative ability. This is particularly true for the creative arts. From a very early age, children love to scribble and draw, and as they grow older to make things out of junk materials and modelling clay. As soon as they have access to paints they quickly go on to the exploration of colour and pattern, and, provided they escape undue interference from well-meaning adults, their love for the visual arts goes with them into primary school, where up to the age of 11 most children name art as their favourite lesson. Music is also a great attraction. Young children love to make sounds with whatever instruments are put into their hands, and take great pleasure in joining with adults to sing nursery rhymes. They have a similar love for story-making, listening while others read stories to them and soon inventing their own. Acting, dressing up and games of make-believe are also part of childhood.

Sadly, as we grow older, most of us forget our love for creativity, and slip all too easily into the habit of claiming that we can't draw, can't sing and can't do anything to express what, whether we like it or not, remains an instinctive part of ourselves. Why is expressing this creative urge so important for our psychological well-being? The first of the many good reasons is that the ability to create is one of the major qualities that distinguishes us as a species, and allowing it to lie idle denies us a valuable outlet for our emotional energies and for expressing and coming to terms with many of the stresses and setbacks of life. A second good reason is that creativity helps us contact progressively deeper levels of the unconscious mind. Carl Jung (1971) refers to the unconscious as 'the personification of the soul', by which we can take him to mean the sum total of our psychological and spiritual life, a life of which the conscious mind is only the most readily accessible fragment. Failure to contact deeper levels of this life means that we go through our days without even realizing these levels are there. The creative urge, which springs from these hidden levels, not only helps reveal aspects of them to us but can help lead as back into them and to even deeper and more comprehensive dimensions of ourselves.

Vision, Creativity and Memory

This is particularly true of creative acts involving vision. As mentioned earlier in the book, the human race made pictures before it developed the written word, and pictures remain an essential part of the language of the unconscious, particularly of the collective unconscious, where they are closely linked to symbolism and the archetypes. Visualization meditations are an excellent way of helping us get back in touch with our creative abilities. They are also an excellent way of helping us develop our powers of memory, especially of visual memory. Watch a very small child drawing a picture of a house. The picture lacks some details, but it is recognizable as a house because it has a front wall, a door, windows and a roof, the essential features of a house. Similarly, watch a child drawing a person. Again some of the details are lacking, but there are a head with eyes and a mouth, arms and legs, and sometimes fingers and a body. The essentials are there. How does the child know how to draw a house and a person even when he does not have a house or a person in front of him? The answer lies in the visual memory. The child has seen houses and people, and the unconscious carries a memory of them that can be transferred to paper. As he or she grows older, more and more detail is included until quite soon we are probably commenting that the results are better than we could produce ourselves.

We shall be dealing with ways of accessing the deeper unconscious through visualization meditations in the final chapter so we can leave the subject until then, but this is the place to discuss the crucial importance of memory and its links to visualization. Memory is one of our most precious possessions. Without memory, we would not only be unable to deal with everyday life, we would quickly lose much of our sense of self. We are in many ways the product of our life history and the memories that it carries. When we wake each morning, the consciousness remembers who we were when we went to sleep, and it is this remembrance that tells us we are still the same person and leads us to expect we will continue to be the same person. People who lose their memories as a result of injury or illness literally also lose themselves.

Actually, we are probably wrong to speak of 'losing' the memory. The fact that people sometimes recover their memories even after lengthy periods of amnesia following accident or illness suggests that memory may never really be lost. It is perhaps more accurate to say that for a time it has not been possible to access it. Even in ordinary life we know that long-forgotten memories can suddenly be recalled in response to appropriate triggers. For example, we may see a faded photograph of a long-forgotten holiday when we were a small child, and suddenly detail after detail of the holiday come flooding back. Or we may look at a book that we are convinced we have not read, and a single sentence abruptly brings back the plot and the characters and we realize that we enjoyed the book some years ago. In examples such as these, the memories concerned have lain buried in the unconscious, perhaps because they were never needed, but when the moment is right they reappear. The same thing can happen under hypnosis. When in a deeply hypnotized state, memories from very early childhood can frequently be recalled. We know these memories can be accurate from the results of experiments in which the hypnotized subject is asked to tell us on which day of the week a certain birthday fell. Birthdays are so important to small children that when they occur the child will always know the day of the week concerned, and although this knowledge will be consciously forgotten as time passes, the fact that it is recalled under hypnosis confirms that long-forgotten early memories can indeed be accurate, and can re-emerge after being stored unused for many years in the deeper levels of the unconscious.

There is some doubt among psychologists as to whether or not we can 'train' the memory by engaging in memorizing exercises, but there is no doubt that we can lessen or even prevent the decline in memory that tends to take place as we grow older if we make sure to use our memories effectively. For example, all too often we don't make proper use of our powers of recall. The more we try to remember something, the more stubbornly it eludes us, when in fact one of the effective exercises when a wanted name or fact refuses to come to mind is simply to instruct the unconscious to find it for us. The instruction must be clear and precise, such as 'I want you to find the name of the author of … for me,' or 'Please get me the exact amount I paid for … ' Having given the instruction, the matter is then put out of the conscious mind and no deliberate attempt is made to recall it. One goes on with other things, then suddenly and of its own accord the wanted fact comes to mind. This demonstrates that the unconscious does indeed possess its own search engine, which can work perfectly effectively without any help from the conscious mind – in fact the latter can impede the process of recall, rather as we might impede a computer search engine if we keep blocking its activity by searching for the wanted material ourselves.

Another reason why we do not use our memories effectively is

Box 9: Kim's Game

In the East, the training the disciple receives from his or her guru includes the skills of looking, remembering and visualizing (training in the Western mystery traditions follows a similar path). Rudyard Kipling's book *Kim* touches on this training, and in particular gives details of what has become known as 'Kim's Game'.

The game involves placing an assortment of everyday objects on a table or a tray, and giving the player one minute or less (dependent on age) to view them. At the end of this time, he or she has to go into another room and write down as many of the objects as can be recalled (the television game that passes objects to be remembered on a conveyer belt in front of a contestant derives from the same idea).

Dependent on the age of the player around 30 objects are usually used. The aim is to *visualize* the array of objects, and to recall this visualization afterwards. Other memory tricks, such as trying to associate each object with a different piece of furniture within one's own home, work much less well because time is too short. In addition, they destroy the main object of the exercise which is to visualize.

The experienced visualizer simply looks briefly at the objects as if taking a photograph of them, and recalls them effortlessly.

that we fail to pay proper attention to things in the first place. Especially as we grow older, we often have so much on our minds that our thoughts are somewhere else instead of being centred in the moment. All meditation practices help us to train our powers of attention and to prevent our minds from wandering, and the practices associated with visualization are particularly effective. Visualization teaches us to look. As mentioned earlier, when we look at something our eyes usually flicker almost continuously from one area of it to another. Visualization teaches us to keep the eyes still, to concentrate upon a point selected as the main focus. Once this has been taken in, the point of focus shifts purposefully, and the eyes then remain still again while this new area is properly absorbed visually. Then the eyes move again, and another area is closely studied. In this way the whole of the image is taken in and retained. Instead of restless movement, the eyes remain under full control, and move only as and when necessary.

Artists and the Magical Act of Seeing

The reason why artists are able to draw accurate representations of objects from memory is that they have looked properly at these objects in the first place. The artist is in love with vision, with shapes and colours, with the magical act of seeing. When photography first became recognized as an accurate and reliable way of capturing images there were many who said it meant that painting was now dead. After all, there was no need to try to reproduce things in paint when the job could be done effectively and much more rapidly with film. However, the people who prophesied the death of painting were wrong. Painting is more highly prized than ever, and paintings sell for much higher prices than photographs. The reason is that artists and cameras look at things in different ways. The camera sees only the surface of things, the artist looks at them much more deeply. The camera sees things in an instant, in the opening and closing of a shutter and the burst of a flashlight, the artist studies them at length, looking and learning. The camera catches a moment in time, the artist works outside time. The camera captures only the present, the artist captures the history that creates the present. A photograph, for all the skill of the photographer, is made by the object that is photographed, a painting is made not by the object but by the creative mind of the artist. Thus, unlike the photograph, the painting is rarely intended as an accurate representation of how an object appears to a camera. It is a representation of how the human mind *sees* that object, for the human mind brings the accumulated memories of a lifetime of seeing, along with their many and varied associations. For the artist, a painting is an imaginative experience, and this experience appeals to us because it resonates with our own imagination in a way that a photograph so rarely can.

We do not all aspire to be artists, but the ability to pay attention to what we see, and then subsequently to bring it back to life through the use of our visual imagination adds another dimension to experience. Because vision is our dominant sense, and because pictures, and not language, lie at the deepest level of our minds, the ability to recall what we see sharpens the efficient use of memory, and helps us to retain this efficiency even when we reach the point in adult life where the powers of memory would otherwise decline.

To develop our powers of visualization as a way of helping us use our memories effectively, we should make sure we know how to look. As already made clear, looking involves the patience and self-discipline to take in what we see, to focus properly on the visual experience. But there is another secret known to all artists, namely to focus on things without letting language intrude. This means avoiding the habit of always naming the things at which we are looking and then dismissing them from our minds as if we have somehow understood them. Once we give something a name all too often we rob it of its individuality. For example, we call something a 'tree', but there are countless million trees in the world, all of them different. The tree we are looking at is not just a tree, it is *this* tree, in all its uniqueness, and there has never been another tree quite like it. In reality it is a magical pattern of shapes and colours and of empty spaces between the shapes and colours. The empty spaces also make shapes that border and define the leaves and the branches, just as the leaves and the branches define the empty spaces. If we look at things in this way we begin to see the whole visual world as a subtle interlacing of shapes, some of them composed of form and some of them composed of space. Colours also play a vital part in this pattern, colours that are constantly changing in response to the play of light and shadow. Movement too plays its role. Nature is very rarely still – even the slightest breeze sets a tree in motion, creating a dance that animates life with a special kind of joy. If we want to visualize correctly, we have to be able to take in and then 'see' in imagination things as they *really* are, and not as our customary and cursory way of glancing at the world has led us to *believe* they are.

The ability to look is also greatly helped if we try drawing what we have seen. We loved to draw when we were children, and recapturing this love is not difficult, provided we don't allow that old enemy, destructive criticism, to intrude. Criticism of this kind effectively gets in the way of both enjoyment and of progress. Drawing is one of the most pleasant and relaxing – and I have to say therapeutic – pastimes there is, and it costs next to nothing to do. Trees, faces and flowers are among the most popular subjects, but houses, mountains, the human figure, clouds and virtually anything that catches the eye can be chosen. Initially, try drawing things that are in front of you, but visualization is particularly helped by drawing things from memory. The more closely we look at something, the more likely we are to be able to recall it when we pick up our pencil. Once the drawing is complete, we can check up on how close it is to the real thing. Accuracy is often less important than the ability to capture a good impression. If the drawing arouses something of the same feelings in us as the scene itself, then we know we are making good progress. A good test is to put the drawing on one side and only look at it again some days later. This allows us to see it with fresh eyes, almost as if it is the work of someone else, and the result often surprises us by its quality. But always draw freely, thinking not of the result but of the enjoyment of the moment.

Drawing as Self-Discovery

Remember that we are talking about drawing not just for its own sake but because it helps self-discovery and the expression of deeper feelings. Free drawing is far more revealing than laboured attempts at getting something 'right' (clients in therapy who find it difficult to articulate or even to access their real feelings, often succeed in doing so if they are asked to draw them). But remember the quartet of shapes, spaces, colours (use coloured pencils) and the suggestion of movement, along with the advice not to constantly attach labels to the things we see instead of looking at them as they are. Betty Edwards, in one of the best short books aimed at showing people who protest they can't draw just how wrong they are (Edwards 1981), emphasizes a similar point. Don't think, just *see*. For example, our knowledge that a cube is made up of right angles gets in the way of drawing what we actually see since, owing to perspective, what we see are not right angles at all. Only by drawing what we see, instead of what we think we see, are we likely to achieve a likeness of a cube. Another example is a pair of spectacles, which most of us can't make look realistic when we are trying to draw a face. Our knowledge of what spectacles *are* prevents us from seeing how spectacles *appear* when they are on the face of the wearer. Some great Impressionist painters use this confusion between knowing and seeing in their work, but they are well aware of what they are doing. If we look at the work of Picasso, before he went on to become a cubist, we find that he was a superb draughtsman and knew perfectly well how to draw what he saw. Only those who know the rules know how to break them!

As the title of her book *Drawing on the Right Side of the Brain* suggests, Betty Edwards considers that our tendency to draw what we know, instead of what we see, is owing to the fact that we are using the left side or hemisphere of our brain instead of the right. The left side of the brain is involved with both our use of language and of analytical thinking/logic, and thus insists on telling us what things are ('It's a chair', 'It's a cube', 'They are spectacles', 'It's an orange', 'It's a book' etc.) and claims that because it can name them it 'knows' exactly how to draw them. When it tries, its attempt is so unlike the real object that we give up drawing in disgust. By contrast, the right side of the brain is more involved with spatial relationships, patterns, and visual perception. Like the left hemisphere, it too is involved in thinking and in problem solving, but thinking and problem solving that is largely language-free (it is perfectly possible to think without language, using pictures, the visual memory and the ability to see how things relate to each other in form and space). Not surprisingly, Betty Edwards emphasizes that we must drop left-brain thinking when trying to draw, and instead get into our right brain. Put simply, this means doing what we have already emphasized, that is putting our knowledge of what things are to one side, and focusing instead on what we actually see in front of us.

Shifting into the Right Brain

In her book, Betty Edwards gives a number of exercises designed to help us shift into this right-brain consciousness, one of the most important of which is to present ourselves with a task that the left brain can't do, such as drawing an object or copying a picture that is placed upside down. When a familiar object or picture is placed upside down, the left brain cannot make 'sense' of it. Instead of something well known and recognizable, all that appears to the eye is an abstract arrangement of shapes and spaces. In order to draw this arrangement one must simply draw what one sees. When the task is finished and the drawing is turned right way up, the surprise is that it represents a good, or even very good, likeness of the object or picture concerned.

One of my own favourite exercises is to try drawing with the wrong hand. The emphasis is upon drawing freely, without checking for accuracy, as the aim is simply to free up the natural ability to draw (or to paint if your prefer). One can either draw from memory, or use an object or picture right or wrong way up, and when the drawing is finished it is often found to possess a freshness, a vigour and an immediacy reminiscent of the work of a child, which is a good sign that this natural ability is being released. On reverting to the correct hand, one aims at retaining and using the same frame of mind. If one slips back into the bad old logical and tentative habits, another session with the wrong hand helps correct things.

The more you practise exercises like this, the more they encourage you to look at the world around you. Another of Betty Edwards' recommendations is to draw the *spaces around* shapes and forms rather than the shapes and forms themselves. The spaces are abstract whereas the shapes and forms are concrete, thus the spaces do not have associations with words and concepts. When I first tried to draw the shapes around objects, rather than the objects themselves, I was on holiday in France and found it a revelation. The world became a visual experience in which space and form and even (though the cause escaped me) time were linked together in a flowing seamless garment of reality. This is, of course, how the world and our own existence actually *is*. There are no boundaries between objects and the space around them, no boundaries between what is seen and what is unseen, no boundaries between the flow of past, present and future. All things are part of the whole, and although in the West we grow up with the notion that we are somehow separate from the rest of existence, solitary units set down like chess pieces in a world that we only dimly understand, nothing could be further from the truth.

Once the nature of this unity is recognized through visual experience, it opens up other insights into our relationship with the world around us. For example, the realization that the substances of which our bodies are made are no different from the substances in the outside world. The iron, the copper, the water, the oxygen in our lungs and in our blood, everything we have and that we are, is no different from these substances in other beings and in the ground under our feet. Our very survival depends upon taking the outside world – the air we breath, the water we drink, the food we eat – into ourselves. Similarly, in a psychological sense, the nature of much of our inner reality is created by the experiences given to us by the outside world, just as our way of relating to this world is largely determined by our inner reality. Try as we might, we cannot separate any aspect of the world from the whole, and see it as having independent existence.

Unity and Interdependence

Our failure to recognize the fact of this unity, and the interdependence to which it gives rise, is the main reason for our problems as a species. It is responsible for our constant desire to change things to suit our own convenience, to 'develop' the natural world into a concrete nightmare, to exhaust its resources, to exterminate much of its biodiversity, and to impose our way of being and of thinking upon the rest of existence. This desire to change the world to suit ourselves is especially true of our Western culture. An Eastern sage once said that the problem with Western man is that he cannot sit quietly in his own room. Indeed, Western man cannot. Whether as individuals or as a culture, we always want to invade the rooms of others, and wreck them in the process. We exercise power as a way of confirming what we mistakenly believe is our separate identity, to prove we are right by trying to prove others are wrong, to take what does not belong to us because we believe we have a right to it. Increasingly, with the daily assault upon us of the artificial electronic world of the media and of the latest technological gimmickry, we are losing what was left of our ability to *look* at the natural world around us, and understand its message.

It would be unrealistic to suppose that all the ills of modern humankind could be solved by remembering the ability to look and to visualize, but it is certainly true that we will not solve them

Box 10: Searching for Existence

We are told as children that one of the major differences between ourselves and animals is that we are conscious of ourselves (self-conscious). This is rather foolish for two reasons; firstly, we do not know whether animals are self-conscious or not, and base our dismissal of their self-consciousness on such flimsy evidence as their inability to recognize themselves in mirrors. Secondly, we do not know much about this 'self' of which we are supposed to be conscious. Buddhism, in fact, rejects the idea of a 'self' as anything more than a learned construction which is subject to constant change.

However, we are certainly aware of our own existence, and can refer to this as a self if we wish. But the seeker after inner wisdom wants to know more than this. What is it to 'exist', what indeed is 'life'? The answer must of course lie within ourselves, as we are the ones who exist, the ones who are alive, and we are therefore the answer to our own question. Can you visualize what it would mean *not* to exist? Visualizing darkness, emptiness, nothingness is not enough, since you are still there to do the visualizing. Now, how would you visualize existence? Imagine you are an artist and are painting a picture of existence, what would it be like? Would it be abstract or figurative? What colours would it use? What emotions would it seek to convey?

Allow the unconscious to do the work for you. Put the conscious mind to one side and let the unconscious take over. If no images arise, this is an interesting discovery in itself. Instruct the unconscious to continue with the task even when the consciousness is engaged on other things. Then note what may come through from time to time, perhaps in dreams, perhaps while you are awake. If you wish, keep a drawing book and allow the unconscious to draw or paint these images. Don't judge the results or allow the critical conscious mind to intrude. Simply note what is happening.

without this ability. *Looking* at the beauties of the natural world enables us to acquire a wealth of visual memories that help to refine our sensitivities, and renders us increasingly aware of our relationship to this world. The clearer our powers of visualization, the clearer these memories become, and the closer we are to recognizing, understanding and accepting the mystery and the beauty of the world. I began my career as a child psychologist, and quickly became conscious of the joy with which small children greet the world. Provided they are blessed with a loving and caring family, their eyes light up over the simplest things. Their attention is caught by movement and by shapes and colours, by the light and shade of trees and sunlight, the sound of water and of the wind. To them the world is a magical place, and its mystery is present in everything they see and touch and hear. As the years pass, they lose much of this early delight, primarily because we teach them to make 'sense' of the world by using their brains instead of their eyes, and substituting theory and other people's ideas (important as these are in their place) for direct experience. The world loses it mystery because everything is presented as if ultimately it can be explained. The fact that we do not know where life comes from or where it goes is rapidly forgotten, as is the fact that we do not even know where our own thoughts come from, or what this mysterious thing we choose to call ourselves actually is. Children are taught to look to others for answers, to look outwards instead of inwards. They are not told that it is for each of us to discover the nature of our own being, and to find the hidden door and the pathway that leads beyond it to the goal of all our searching.

Chapter 6

Visualization and the Magical World of Dreams

The Universal Nature of Dreaming

As we said earlier in the book, we all visualize in dreams, and research indicates that we dream every night, for up to a quarter of our total hours of sleep. When people are awakened in sleep laboratories during REM (Rapid Eye Movement) sleep, a phase of light sleep from which paradoxically it is more difficult to be aroused than it is from deep sleep, they almost invariably report they were dreaming. Typically they give details of dream events, even though they may be people who normally claim they never dream. In REM sleep, so called because the eyes move behind the closed eyelids as if following what is happening in the dream, dreams tend to be vivid and lifelike. We dream less often in deeper, non-REM sleep, and these dreams tend to be slower, greyer, and usually briefer, with less action.

Psychologists are still not sure why we dream. One theory is that dreams reflect the brain's attempt to process the information acquired during the day and to discard anything unimportant (hence their illogical and frequently confused nature), rather as a computer discards unwanted material when we go off-line at the end of the day. The other major theory is quite different, and holds that dreams arise more often from the unconscious, and that they constitute a symbolic language that, if properly interpreted, gives us revealing information about our inner life. The first of these two theories argues that we should not try to remember our dreams, as remembering them would mean hanging on to unwanted and meaningless mental clutter. By contrast, the second theory insists that we should not only try to remember our dreams but should seek their symbolic meaning. Some of the dream symbols are personal to ourselves (in the way, for example, that a particular armchair remembered from childhood might symbolize comfort and security) and arise from the complex network of associations that we build up during our life. Others (such as the cross or the crescent, the wise old man or the divine child) are part of the universal symbolic language that occurs across cultures and represents shared archetypal energies (see Fontana 1993 and 1994). In terms of this second theory, some dreams come from the personal unconscious, while those with universal symbols come from the collective unconscious, and it is sometimes proposed that dreams may even come from a source outside ourselves, as explained later.

The second of these two theories is associated with the work of Freud, Jung and of psychoanalytical and transpersonal psychologists and counsellors, while the former theory is favoured by those physiologists and biologists who prefer to explain all mental activity in terms of physical brain processes. One way of deciding between the two theories is to study your own dreams. Do they seem like the brain processing daily events and discarding anything that is unwanted, or do they seem like the dramatization of many of the hopes and fears, memories and preoccupations, desires and longings of our inner life? As will become apparent from this chapter, my personal experience with my own dreams and with my work in psychotherapy and psychological counselling leaves me in no doubt which of the two theories is the more appropriate.

Visual Experience and Inspiration in Dreams

For many people the most striking feature of dreams is that they do not follow the logic of waking life. We may find ourselves in dreams to be younger or older than we really are. We may see ourselves in a mirror and find we look quite different from our waking self, perhaps an idealized version of it. Our relationships with others may bear no resemblance to those we have in waking life, and we may have close encounters with people we never meet outside dreams. This lack of waking logic may extend to the dream world itself. The house in which we live in our dreams may be nothing like our real house. Objects may have the habit of changing into something else even while we look at them. Familiar places may look unfamiliar. Familiar objects may be confused with unfamiliar ones in a kind of surrealist melange. We may find ourselves in enchantingly beautiful surroundings that we have never seen or imagined in waking life, or in ugly or frightening ones. And so on. Yet perhaps the strangest thing of all is that none of this may strike us as odd while we are dreaming. We accept it all as if it is real, and on waking it may sometimes take us a little time to readjust to reality.

What does all this tell us about our powers of visualization, for dream experiences are visualizations, every bit as compelling and convincing – if not more so – than those we experience in waking life? The first thing is that, even if dreams come only from our own minds, they demonstrate that we have quite extraordinary powers of dramatic imagination. We tend to take these powers for granted because we are so used to the idea of dreaming. But if we pause and think about our night-time adventures we realize that often they rival any novel for interest and invention. Not surprisingly, many writers have claimed that their best ideas have indeed come from their dreams. Robert Louis Stevenson, author of *Treasure Island* and many other classics for both adults and children, claimed that while dreaming little people – who he called his Brownies – actually deliberately constructed many of his plots for him. One of this best-known stories, *The Strange Case of Dr Jekyll and Mr Hyde,* was given to him in this way. Samuel Taylor Coleridge's wonderful poem *Kubla Khan* came to him in a dream, and when he was interrupted while writing it he found himself unable to complete it so that sadly only an inspired fragment remains. The poet William Blake, who made the greater part of his living as an engraver, reported that a new method of copper engraving was given to him in a dream by his dead brother, who he claimed often visited him in sleep. Among other famous writers who have reported that their work has been inspired by dreams are the poet John Keats, the novelists Sir Walter Scott, Edgar Alan Poe and H G Wells, and the dramatist and novelist J B Priestly.

Musicians have also reported receiving inspiration in dreams. One of the best-known examples is the 18th-century Italian composer Giuseppe Tartini, famous for his violin pieces. Tartini claimed that the devil (some might prefer to identify the visitant as the Greek god Pan, an archetypal symbol of the natural world and known for his music) appeared in a dream while Tartini was staying in the monastery at Assisi. The devil picked up Tartini's violin and played an unknown sonata that Tartini described as 'surpassing the wildest flights of my imagination'. When he awoke he endeavoured to recall the music and to write it down (the much-loved *Le Trillo de Devilola,* or *The Devil's Trill*), and although he felt his memory of it was only partial he still considered it the best thing he ever wrote.

Inspiration in dreams does not come only to writers and musicians. A number of eminent scientists have also reported receiving some of their best ideas visually in dreams. A good example is the German chemist Friedrich Kekulé, who in 1890 reported that his discovery of the molecular structure of benzene in 1865 – a discovery that provided the foundation for modern molecular chemistry – had come to him in symbolic form in a dream. René Descartes, another major name in the development of modern science, was inspired in his early work by three dreams that changed the whole course of his thinking and that he considered represented guidance from God. Niels Bohr, a key figure in the development of quantum physics, is reported as dreaming, while a student, that he stood on the surface of a sun with planets whirling past, each of them attached to the sun by a thin filament. On awakening, he recognized that this was the long-sought model of the atom. Accounts of Bohr's dream vary a little, and it may be that he had more than one dream revelation, but it is interesting that three of the founders of modern science (Kekulé – chemistry, Bohr – physics, and Descartes – the philosophy of science) all received inspiration from dream visions (see Brook 1983, Fontana 1990).

One explanation for inspiration of this kind is that the scientists had each been puzzling over scientific problems during waking life, and that the dreaming mind simply organized their thinking more effectively and came up with the solution. This explanation is preferred by orthodox scientists, despite the fact that, if true, it disposes of the first of the two theories given above, namely that dreams are simply the brain dumping unwanted information and are best not remembered. However, if we turn to the theory that dream visualizations are much more than a reworking of waking thoughts, we find that cultures from both West and East have believed over the centuries that many dreams are a portal to much deeper inner experiences, and that some are indeed given to us by God or the gods as a way of providing warnings and guidance.

Warnings and Messages

Most of the world's sacred books contain accounts of warning and messages from God or from the gods. In the Bible, Joseph was warned 'of God in a dream' of the dangers to the infant Christ. Pilate's wife cautioned Pilate to take no action against Christ 'for I have suffered many things this day in a dream because of him'. In the Old Testament God tells Aaron and Miriam that if there is a true prophet among the Israelites 'I ... will speak unto him in a dream'. Job announces that 'when deep sleep falleth upon men ... then He openeth the ears of men and sealeth their instruction', while Joseph became rich and powerful by virtue of his understanding and interpretation of dreams. The Koran tells us that Mohammed was taken up to heaven by the angel Gabriel in a dream, and that much of the Koran was dictated to him in dreams, and that on many occasions he was visited by Gabriel during sleep. Buddhists, Hindus, Jains – indeed virtually all the psycho-spiritual traditions, including the Shamanic cultures of the Americas, Africa and Siberia – have all emphasized dreams as a doorway to other worlds and to other forms of knowledge, and stressed the importance of learning ways of controlling and using dreams.

All these traditions emphasize that dreams can mislead as well as provide true guidance. The ancient Greeks believed that dreams came through two doorways, the Gates of Horn and the Gates of Ivory, the former being true and the latter false dreams. One way of ensuring true dreams was to spend the night at temples or special shrines where priests could be consulted on matters of dream interpretation. In addition to the many traditions that believe dreams can give guidance and predict the future, the Nyingma school (the oldest of the sects of Tibetan Buddhism) teaches that dreams are a dress rehearsal for death. If we are able to gain control over dreams, by practices described below, then we will be able to gain some control over the processes of dying and of what happens to us in the afterlife, the lower levels of which the Nyingma teach are also a kind of dream world.

Dreams and the Collective Unconscious

Although Freud did much to establish the importance of dreams and their relationship with deep levels of our own mind, it was primarily owing to him that we in the West abandoned the idea that dreams could come to us from a source outside ourselves.

Freud (1953) saw dreams primarily as dramatized wish-fulfil-ments of the repressed desires and neurotic anxieties hidden in our personal unconscious, and this is still very much the view of Freudians. However, Carl Jung took the view (and this was the main reason for his break with Freud) that although many dreams arise from our personal unconscious, others – which he called great or grand dreams – come from the collective unconscious, that part of the mind that shares the inherited psychological and spiritual tendencies of the human race, and that appears receptive to much more than our own life experience and also perhaps to influences from beyond our own minds.

Freud and Jung were giant figures in the development of the psychology of the inner life. Both wrote prodigiously, with collected works that, for both men, run into more than 20 weighty volumes. Psychoanalysts certainly find that working with dreams often reveals far more about people's psychological problems than any other procedure. For many years the balance of opinion was tipped towards Freud's ideas but currently there is increasing interest in the work of Jung, primarily because he accepted – and used in his psychotherapeutic practice – the concept of a spiritual dimension to life. Thus he appeals to the spiritual urges and longings felt by large numbers of people. Jung's deep experience of his own inner life (see Jung 1963), together with his extensive work as a psychotherapist, convinced him that no psychology of the human mind is complete unless it takes the spiritual dimension into account, and for him dreams were one of the most effective ways of contacting this dimension, which is found in and through and perhaps beyond the collective unconscious.

In the context of dreams we must also take into account the *hypnogogic* and the *hypnopompic* states, both of which are of great importance in any study of visualization. What are these states? Do you sometimes have the experience, just as you are drifting into sleep, of seeing vivid pictures flashing before your closed eyes, sometimes in a dreamlike sequence, sometimes as separate images? And do you sometimes have similar experiences as you emerge from sleep? The former state is known as the *hypnogogic* and the latter as the *hypnopompic*. One of the frustrating features of both states is that the images they give us are usually too fleeting to be committed to memory. When we are properly awake we know they happened, but their content eludes us. However, those who can recall them testify to the fact that they often include creative insights that do not occur in waking hours. A good example is that of the great surrealist painter Salvador Dali, who trained himself to remain in the half-world between waking and sleeping in which these images appear, and who used many of them in his paintings. As mentioned previously, one of Dali's methods for staying in this half-world without falling into sleep was to prop a fork below his chin. Should his head begin to nod forward he would feel the pricking of the fork, and wake sufficiently to return to the hypnogogic state.

Lucid Dreaming

Another area of dreaming relevant to visualization is the so-called lucid dream. This is a dream in which we suddenly become aware that the dream really is just a dream. Thus, instead of experiencing the dream as if it is analogous to waking reality, we know that we are in a quite different state, and can even take control of the dream and decide what to do with it. For example, we might decide to visit a beautiful place, or a wise man or woman. Once the decision is taken, the dream takes us to where we want to go. We do not have to 'imagine' the place or the person concerned, the dream does it for us, just as if there is another creative mind, separate and distinct from our own, that like a clever dramatist is staging the whole thing. The reality of lucid dreams has been well documented through scientific research, in particular following on from the work of Dr Stephen LaBerge who, in the sleep laboratory at Stanford University in the USA, developed a method by which the dreamer could signal – for example by a pre-arranged pattern of REM – that although still asleep he or she has control of the dreaming state (LaBerge 1985 and 1990).

Some people have frequent lucid dreams, others have them rarely or never. However, for those who do have them the experience is unforgettable. Colours become immediately more vivid, and the boundary between waking and dreaming experience disappears. We can, for example, ask for answers to questions about ourselves and our personal problems, or for help in arriving at solutions to difficulties we may be encountering in daily life, or for creative ideas to help us in our work. However, there is no guarantee that we will receive answers as, at the moment they are about to be given, the dream sometimes frustratingly refuses to stay lucid. We drop back into ordinary dreaming, and our access to what

---

Box 11: Inducing Lucid Dreams

One of the oldest techniques for inducing successful lucid dreams, and for allowing consciousness to run continually through waking and sleeping, depends upon the ability to watch oneself falling asleep. This is not as difficult as it sounds, although initial attempts may result in periods of prolonged wakefulness. All that it requires is to be aware of gradually falling asleep, an awareness of which we are often conscious when struggling to stay awake while sitting on the front row at a boring speech or lecture.

Once nearing the actual border between waking and sleeping, visualize a pleasant, tranquil scene of some kind, and at the last moment before sleep overtakes you, step into it.

When you have perfected this technique, consciousness runs continually from waking to sleeping, and you find yourself in the visualized scene, in what is in fact a lucid dream.

---

seems like higher wisdom is lost. At other times the answers are given but consist of symbols that we may find difficult to interpret, or the dream even refuses to take us to the person or the place where the answers can be given. But there is no doubt that lucid dreaming not only adds an exciting new dimension to our experience of our own minds, it opens up very real opportunities for exploring this dimension and for valuable insights into self-understanding.

Out-of-body Experiences

In many instances, lucid dreams also seem to facilitate what are known as out-of-body experiences (OBEs), those experiences in which the consciousness appears to leave the physical body (which may sometimes even be seen asleep on the bed from a vantage point elsewhere in the bedroom). Some people who have these experiences report that, during them, they usually appear to stay within their normal environment and may, as we have just said, actually see their sleeping physical bodies, while others find themselves taken to places of breathtaking beauty that previously they had neither seen nor imagined. Yet others find themselves in an environment that appears to be a clever, if inaccurate, copy of our own world, in which familiar places are seen yet with their details subtly altered. After a time, in all three experiences, there is a return to the physical body, often as if pulled back by some force, usually invisible but said at times to resemble a silken cord, perhaps analogous to that mentioned in Ecclesiastes 12:6 where death is spoken of as the time when man 'goeth to his long home' and 'the silver cord [is] loosed'. One explanation for this invisible force is that it is the connection between the externalized consciousness and the physical body, and that indeed this connection is 'loosed' at death.

Sceptics claim that consciousness does not really leave the body during out-of-body experiences and that they are simply imagination. One way of checking if this is so is to discover if individuals can obtain information, while supposedly out of their bodies, that they could not have come upon while in their bodies. The most impressive experiment of this kind was carried out some years ago by Professor Charles Tart, one of the world's leading researchers into seemingly paranormal phenomena, at the University of California at Davis. Professor Tart was fortunate in finding a young woman (referred to as Miss Z to protect her anonymity) who claimed the ability to leave her body at will during sleep and to view objects in the real world while doing so. Professor Tart brought her to his sleep research laboratory at the university, where she slept for four nights, carefully monitored at all times to ensure that she did not leave her bed. On a ledge in the room, above her sight, Tart placed a five-figure random number, unknown to Miss Z, which he changed each night. On the first three nights Miss Z reported being out of her body, but unable to orientate herself sufficiently in the unfamiliar room to find the number. On the fourth night, however, she managed to read the number, and reported it correctly to Professor Tart. The number – 25132 – is surely one of the most famous in the whole of psychical research, and it is unfortunate that orthodox scientists have studiously ignored the results of this extraordinary scientific experiment (Tart 1989).

The odds against getting a five-figure random number correct with only one guess are 100,000 to 1 against. This makes it clear that her correct answer was so unlikely to have been a lucky guess that we are safe in regarding the experience to have been paranormal. In addition, Miss Z was connected to an electro-encephalograph to measure her brain waves during the hours of sleep, and Professor Tart reports that her alpha brain waves, typical of a sleeping state, slowed by one and a half cycles from normal during her successful OBE, a highly unusual occurrence that provided further evidence that something anomalous had taken place.

Some critics, while accepting that Miss Z could not have read the number by normal means, have argued that, instead of being out of her body, she had read it clairvoyantly. If this were the case then, although the experiment remains of great interest, it does not add to the evidence that at least some people can leave their bodies during sleep. The answer to these critics is to take account of Miss Z's description of own experiences. It seems fair to suggest that she is a better judge of these experiences than critics who have never themselves read a five-figure random number either while out of the body or by clairvoyance. Miss Z – who had experienced OBEs since childhood – was in no doubt that she was out of her body, and the fact that on the first three nights she found it impossible to orientate herself properly in the unaccustomed surroundings of the sleep laboratory provides further evidence that suggests she knew what was happening to her. In addition, clairvoyance, including the technique known as remote viewing, does not usually produce experiences that can be mistaken for OBEs. Instead, clairvoyants typically receive 'impressions' of the information they hope to obtain. In fact, the mystery traditions have always emphasized the difference between clairvoyance and out-of-body experiences by referring to the latter as *travelling clairvoyance*.

Visualization Exercises for Lucid Dreaming

Having set the scene, we now have to ask if there are visualization exercises that firstly help our dreaming to become more vivid, to reach deeper levels of the unconscious, and to be more readily remembered in the morning. Secondly, we have to ask if visualization exercises can help us experience lucid dreams, and thirdly, whether they can help us have out-of-body experiences. The answer to all three questions is probably yes, although, as with most visualization exercises, we have to be prepared to be patient and to persevere over a period of time.

The prime reason we fail to remember our dreams is that we do not take them seriously enough. In life we tend to forget most readily those things that are not important to us, and in most cases our education has conditioned us to believe that dreams are of no value, and not to be bothered with once we are awake. As we have already made clear, we are in fact one of the very few cultures in world history to have taken this view. In dismissing our dreams we dismiss a large part of our psychological life, and I hope enough has been said in this chapter to indicate that we may suffer as a consequence. The first step therefore is to start reversing the process by *wanting* to remember our dreams. This is then backed up by repeating whenever possible during the day that 'I will remember my dreams', and by focusing on these repetitions last thing at night, while preparing for sleep. The choice of words is up to individuals, but one useful formula just before sleep is – 'I will have very clear and interesting dreams, and when I wake in the morning I will remember them.' This is repeated several times, so that it will be in the mind when sleep actually occurs.

On waking in the morning, it is important to remain in the same position in bed without moving, as this facilitates dream recall. However, no special effort should be made to achieve this recall. Dream memories are often rather like things glimpsed from the corner of the eye. If we turn our head and try to look at them too closely they vanish. Attempt merely to keep the mind open and clear of thoughts. All too often when we awake we start thinking of the day ahead, and in doing so we immediately, if unintentionally, banish the fine fabric of our dreams to the levels of the unconscious from which they arose. Sometimes noting the way you feel when you awake helps in dream recall, since your feelings may be influenced in some way by the dream you were having just before waking up. If memories – however fragmented – come to mind they may trigger others. When it seems clear that nothing further can be recalled, write down what you remember. Keeping a dream diary in this way is an essential aid to dream recall, both because it helps stabilize the dream memories in the mind and because it allows one to look back from time to time to see if patterns, such as recurring themes and symbols, are seen to emerge. It also helps if, occasionally during the day, you think back to your dreams, in the same way you think back to memories of waking life. Don't necessarily make conscious attempts to recall the dreams as visual experiences. To do so is to risk that imagination will take over. Instead, allow visual images to arise of their own accord, just as they did during the dream. If you can, draw some of these images in your dream diary, as this is a great help in prompting memories to stay vivid. As you develop your ability to remember your dreams, so you are likely to find that you recall experiences that appear to arise from deeper levels of the dreaming mind. Instead of easily recognizable fragments from waking life, your dreams will increasingly include scenes and events that have no obvious link with waking life, and it is at this point that some understanding of dream symbolism (a matter to which we return in due course) becomes important.

The faculty for experiencing lucid dreams appear to depend on the ability to *pay attention* in dreams. The more closely we observe dream details, the more likely we are to recognize anomalies, things that don't fit in with waking life, and that prompt the realization that we therefore must be dreaming. Immediately, with a surge of excitement, the dream comes fully alive for us. If you only have one lucid dream in your life, you will remember it as vividly as if it happened yesterday. How does one remain attentive in dreams? The ability often arises naturally as one develops one's powers of attention – of looking – in waking life. As already made clear, this development depends, in part, upon the practice of meditation. The more regularly we meditate, paying attention to our breathing or whatever else is our point of focus, the more we pay attention to everything happening around us in daily life and in dreaming.

As a consequence of this heightened ability to pay attention, we find ourselves noticing, while dreaming, that things are not as they should be. For example, we may notice that a familiar environment or the appearance of people known to us or even our own appearance is changed in some way. Or we may meet animals that talk, or see roadways changing magically into rivers, or find ourselves flying over the countryside, or meeting people who died long ago. The anomalies we encounter in the dream world may be more minor than any of these, yet the more attentive we are the more likely we are to spot them. In one of my early lucid dreams I was walking along a shopping street that for some reason I knew was in Britain, yet all the signs above the shops were in French. This prompted the realization that I must in fact be dreaming, and the dream immediately became lucid.

Another practice for helping the development of lucid dreaming is to ask yourself as often as possible during the day, 'How do I know that this is not a dream?' Look around yourself, and check up. You may decide the answer is that everything appears normal and in its rightful place, or because if you look at something then look away and then back again it has not changed, or because you can pick up a book and read it, or do mathematical calculations, or take a conscious decision such as turning on the tap and putting your hand under the running water. Whatever test you use, the fact that the result is exactly what you expected tells you that you are not in a dream. This reality testing, as it is called, may automatically transfer itself to the dream world after a time, and you can help this to happen by reminding yourself as you drift into sleep that you will try the same test while dreaming. Or if you prefer, you can simply tell yourself as you fall asleep that you will know you are dreaming. This should be done with real intention. In Chapter 7 we refer to the importance of the will in all imaginative practices, and in the case of lucid dreaming we must really *want* to have the experience, and must convey this strong feeling of *wanting* to our unconscious, which will eventually get the message.

Stephen LaBerge, after experimenting with a number of different methods in the sleep laboratory at Stanford University, developed what he called the MILD (Mnemonic Induction of Lucid Dreams) method (LaBerge 1985). Mnemonics refers to those little tricks that, by associating one thing with another, help us remember the things we have to do. An example is the old method of tying a knot in the corner of a handkerchief to remind us of something we have to do, such as calling at the shops on the way home. There is no rational connection between the shops and a knot in a handkerchief, but if we tie the knot while thinking about – and particularly visualizing – calling at the shops the trick works for us (particularly if we are a frequent user of a handker-chief!). The mnemonic recommended by LaBerge in his MILD system is to go over a dream on waking until it is committed to memory (dreams usually fade very quickly unless this is done) and associate it with the thought, 'Next time I am dreaming I will know that I am dreaming.' You then visualize yourself as being back in the dream during the day and before you go to sleep at night, and imagine yourself realizing that you are dreaming. (LaBerge also gives an excellent summary of other methods developed by various dream researchers and various of the psycho-spiritual traditions that prove helpful in inducing lucid dreams.)

Remaining Conscious in Dreams

Apart from the benefits already mentioned, there is another important reason for training ourselves in lucid dreaming. I referred earlier to the fact that the oldest sect of Tibetan Buddhism, the Nyingma, teaches that dreams are a dress rehearsal for death, and that if you can remain conscious during your dreaming you will be able to remain conscious during the act of dying and influence what happens. Lucid dreaming, as you may have guessed, is in fact what is meant by remaining conscious during dreams, and Tibetan Buddhists are not alone in stressing its importance. Hindu traditions teach that there are three mind-states – waking, dreaming, and dreamless sleep – and that consciousness should run continuously through all three. (Consciousness in dreamless sleep would be very much like the deepest states of meditation, in which the attention is clear and focused, and no thoughts arise to disturb the state of what is sometimes called 'calm abiding'.)

Interestingly, the Western mystery or occult traditions have taught something very similar. The loss of consciousness while asleep has always been regarded in these traditions (which were largely based upon the results of direct experience) as a wasted opportunity. It is argued that, in sleep, one has the best chance of making progress on the path of inner development and the quest for the true self, a self that is normally hidden from the conscious mind, and that can only be discovered by following a series of quite clearly defined practices (see Regardie 1972, and Butler 1991), of which gaining control over the hours of sleep is one of the most important. Once this control is gained, the student is able to open the doorway between the conscious and the unconscious minds, and use the latter to gain access to levels of higher wisdom.

Our tendency in the West to dismiss such teachings as unscientific and little more than mere superstition misses an important point. Buddhist, Hindu and Western mystery traditions are centuries old, and based upon deep and careful explorations of the human mind. In the West, much of our emphasis in psychology, and in science generally, has been upon behaviour – what people do – rather than upon what goes on within their minds. This emphasis has been of great value in its way because it means we deal with observable, public evidence. We can all agree, if we watch closely enough, on what people do, whereas we can only know what goes on in their minds if they choose to tell us, and they may intentionally or unintentionally deceive us, or may know very little about their own minds. Science does not like to deal with such levels of uncertainty as this. However, this distrust by science of what goes on in the mind means that we have tended to ignore the inner world, unless we are Freudians or Jungians or transpersonal psychologists. By contrast, Eastern traditions such as Buddhism and

Hinduism have meticulously mapped out inner states of mind and the methods needed to explore them and gain control over them.

Near-Death Experiences

OBEs are closely linked to so-called near-death experiences (NDEs) in which, after recovery from a short period of apparent clinical death, some individuals report having left their bodies and in some instances travelled to what seems to be another world in which deceased friends and relatives may be met, and from where they are sent back, often with great reluctance, into their physical bodies. In some cases these accounts also extend to reports of what was happening around the body while the consciousness was located outside it. Rather like Miss Z in Professor Tart's OBE experiment, these reports may contain accurate details of what was taking place around the body during the period of clinical death, details that could not have been seen while the body was apparently dead and certainly deeply unconscious, and that in any case would not have been visible from the position that the comatose body was occupying.

The important feature both of OBEs and of NDEs is that they appear to show that if consciousness can operate outside the physical body, then it is independent of the body and thus of the physical brain. The relationship between mind and brain is a vitally important issue. If the mind is simply the result of the working of the brain, then it dies when the brain dies, and there is no question of any form of survival after death. On the other hand, if the mind is independent of the brain, and simply works through it, with the brain acting as a link between the non-material mind and the material body, then it would seem that the mind does not die when the brain does. Does brain cause mind, or does mind work through brain? As we saw earlier, recent research has demonstrated that specific areas of the brain are associated with specific mental states, and some scientists conclude from this that these brain areas are therefore responsible for these states. However, such a conclusion is premature, firstly because we have, to date, found no way in which the physical (electrochemical) activity of the brain can give rise to non-physical events such as our thoughts and the many other forms of mental activity. And secondly because OBEs and NDEs provide us with firm evidence that the mind, by which I mean consciousness and the unconscious, appears able to function outside the body, and in some NDEs this is so even when it is known that the brain is literally inactive. For example, Sabom (1998) presents details of a brain operation in which the patient's body temperature was lowered to a level of suspended animation so that her brain could be drained of blood (thus to all intents and purposes switched off) and yet the patient, on resuscitation, not only reported a NDE and the continuation of consciousness but was also able to give some accurate details of what took place in the operating theatre while out of her body.

The NDE appears to show that the materialist's belief that we are no more than biological machines, programmed by evolution and with no higher meaning or purpose to our lives, is just that, a belief. The evidence yielded by OBEs and NDEs is thus of great importance in helping us arrive at an understanding of our own nature. OBEs show us that the mind appears able to leave the body, sometimes in dreams and sometimes even in waking life, and act independently of it and of the physical brain, while NDEs go even further and suggest that the mind can operate independently of the physical brain even during periods of clinical death.

Methods for Inducing OBEs

Most methods for inducing OBE experiences are based upon visualization. The Western mystery traditions, which have used these methods for many centuries, have always insisted that progress in all the deeper levels of self-exploration depends upon two things, firstly *will* and secondly *imagination*. Will implies self-discipline, commitment, patience, and self-belief. One must not only want to succeed, one must *will* oneself to succeed, which means recognizing the importance of what one is trying to do, and single-mindedly working towards it. The same emphasis upon the will is present in the iron-hard discipline of Zen, in the martial arts, in the various Hindu practices of yoga (of which hatha yoga, the yoga of the body, is only one example), and in the monastic disciplines of the Christian Church and of other monastic traditions. However, will alone is not enough, and this is where imagination, particularly visual imagination comes in. The disciplined use of the imagination is considered by these traditions to have a creative power that not only leads to achievement in the outer world but to profound inner changes. Many such changes have already been described in earlier chapters, but even deeper transformative practices are possible.

No one should attempt any of these visualization practices unless he or she has the necessary mental and emotional stability. Imagination can be a two-edged sword, and unless correctly used, and in the context of appropriate psychological health, can lead to problems, such as disturbing hallucinations. If you have any doubt on this score you should certainly take medical advice before attempting any of the practices detailed in this and the following chapter. The same applies if you have any physical problem such as heart trouble that you consider might be adversely affected by them.

There are many different practices developed over the centuries for inducing OBEs, and W E Butler, 40 years after using one of the best known under the guidance of his teacher, describes how the first time he left the body he:

> ...gazed on [my] earthly form lying in deep trance
> on the couch. Whoever has this experience knows in
> a mode of absolute knowledge that he is not the
> physical body with which he has for so long
> identified himself. It is possibly one of the greatest
> experiences which can happen to man.
>
> (Butler 1991)

Butler also emphasizes, as do other writers, that one need have no fear of being unable to return to the physical body. The difficulty (as I can confirm from my own limited experience), 'especially in the early stage, is to *keep out of the physical!*' There seems to be a natural tendency on the part of the physical body to pull the consciousness back into itself (we referred to this earlier in the context of the so-called silken cord that is said to stretch between the physical body and the consciousness). Until this tendency ceases at death, consciousness remains largely confined by the forces of nature within the physical body. In addition, any hint of fear or alarm on the occasions when it is exteriorized seems to result in a rapid return.

The practice used by Butler commences by sitting or lying in a comfortable position (any physical discomfort is likely to interfere with results as it distracts attention), with the eyes open or closed. The next step is to imagine the 'body' that you wish to project. Normally this will be a copy of your physical body. It doesn't matter if the details are not exactly right, but if you do have any difficulties with this you can study a photograph of yourself or your reflection in a mirror beforehand until you have the image firmly in mind. This imaginary body can be dressed as you like (some people find clothes a distraction and prefer to carry out this exercise naked), but not in anything that is likely to spark off memories or associations and get in the way of the next step, which is to imagine the image of yourself actually sitting or lying in front of you and in exactly the same position as yourself. If you are sitting, your imaginary self can either be facing you or have its back to you, and if you are lying it should be above you, so that you are looking directly up at it (again either facing you or with its back to you).

Now try to see the image as if, like you, it is alive (ancient traditions speak of 'transferring some of your vital energy to it'), which many people find easier to do if the image is facing and is smiling with open eyes. The third stage is to imagine the image carrying out actions of some kind, for example standing up, moving about the room, even speaking. The more lifelike these actions appear to be, the better.

The final stage is to will yourself to project your consciousness into the image. Butler stresses that this should be a single act of will, rather than sustained or repeated. It should be an act of confidence, as if you know in advance that success is assured, rather than attempted with gritted teeth (which sends the message to the unconscious that you are unsure if this is going to work). Step forward in imagination and immediately make an imaginative attempt to see and hear from the standpoint of the image. This is the crucial point in the practice, and success may only be achieved after many attempts. Don't make too many attempts at any one time. Trying too often at any one time loses the spontaneous nature of the act of will and of imagination designed to transfer consciousness from the physical body to the visualized body. If after two or three attempts you feel that is enough, remain in meditation and gradually return the visualized figure to rest in front of you, then draw it back into yourself, as if it returns to the imaginative source from which it has arisen.

Drawing the visualized image back into yourself is important. In Tibetan Buddhism there is a practice known as guru yoga in which, very much as in the present exercise, one visualizes a figure sitting just ahead (in this case the Buddha or a revered teacher). Again the imagination is allowed to build up the figure, but this time, instead of trying to project oneself outwards, one allows the figure to rise until it is situated above the crown of the head, and then to descend through the crown until it comes to rest in the heart. The object of the exercise is to absorb into oneself the qualities of the Buddha or of the teacher (or to arouse these latent qualities from within oneself), and it is always stressed that one should never leave the exercise unfinished and with the visualized figure still 'out there'. The visualization is the creation of one's own mind, and must be taken back into one's own mind. Failure to do so can be a way of encouraging hallucinations.

Two Forms of OBE

What happens if the practice works and, like Butler, one finds oneself apparently outside the physical body? The traditions that have practised ways of temporarily leaving the body (see Muldoon, S and Carrington, H, 1987 and 1992) teach that there are two types of OBE. In Type 1, the energy body (said to be the subtle body that sustains the physical body during life, and to which we made reference in Chapter 4), or some part of it, leaves the physical body along with the consciousness (or with the soul body or astral body if you prefer) and sustains the life forces in the physical body through the cord said to connect the two bodies. In Type 2, the energy body remains in the physical body while the consciousness makes its exit alone. The difference in the experiences that one has while out of the body are said to depend upon which of these two forms of the OBE take place. In Type 1, the externalized consciousness remains in the familiar physical world. Often it is able to see the physical body – which usually appears to be in trance or in deep sleep (as in Butler's case quoted earlier) – and the room in which it is lying, although the colours are sometimes described as strangely muted, as if one sees them through a thin mist or fog. In Type 2, the consciousness appears to be located in a copy of the real world, but a rather inexact copy, with familiar objects out of place, for example, or two windows in the room when there should only be one.

This inexact world is said to be the 'astral' world, the lower levels of the next world, created very largely by the thoughts and memories of its inhabitants (although some writers claim that it is our physical world that is an inexact copy of the astral world rather than the other way around). In Type 1, it is possible to move around in the physical world, sometimes even obtaining accurate and previously unknown information (this appears to have been the kind of experience enjoyed by Miss Z in her experiments with Professor Charles Tart described earlier). Some people even report being able to leave their homes and go out into the street. In one of the accounts in my own records, Bob, a man I have known for many years and of whose honesty I am in no doubt, reports that he walks (or rather glides, since there is no impression of effort) through familiar streets, often with the aim of trying to reach a large park some two miles or so from his house. To date he has always been drawn back to his body just before getting there. This sensation of being drawn back to one's body, which appears to be a feature common to the great majority of accounts of OBEs, is yet another indication that such experiences are quite different from remote viewing, the practice in which the individual identifies details clairvoyantly of locations sometimes hundreds if not thousands of miles away.

In a Type 2 OBE, it is reported that it is possible to travel in the astral world rather than in our physical world, and to meet deceased relatives and friends, and sometimes even to visit the Upper Astral, a place of breathtaking beauty where one may meet higher beings. Eventually, and often very much to one's great disappointment, one is compelled to return to the physical body, either because one is sent back or because the pull of the body becomes too strong to resist.

When people give me accounts of their OBEs I always ask if they were aware of being in a 'body', and the answer is usually yes (an answer I can support on the strength of my own limited first-hand experiences). Sometimes the body appears solid and is wearing the same clothes as the physical body, at other times it is wearing different clothes or in some cases no clothes at all, while on other occasions it appears translucent, or to be only partial (e.g. one is aware of only one's head and shoulders).

In a Type 1 OBE, despite the fact that the world looks as solid as in real life, many individuals report they are able to pass through solid objects such as walls and doors, as if their own substance is non-physical. Similarly they report that their hands pass through physical objects that they try to pick up or move, making it difficult or impossible for them to leave objective proof that they have been out of their bodies. Thus Professor Tart's random number test, described earlier, is one of the very few reliable tests that can be used to provide this kind of proof. And here the problem is to find individuals who, like Miss Z, can leave their bodies at will. Such individuals are rare. However, one such individual is Blue Harary, a psychology PhD who, in an experiment conducted by leading researchers Bill Roll and Dr (later Professor) Robert Morris, was asked while out of his body to leave the parapsychology laboratory where he was being supervised by Bill Roll and travel to his own apartment in order to see if his pet cat would detect his presence. The cat was enclosed in a special box, and Dr Morris was on hand to record the amount of time it spent at each end of the box. During Blue Harary's OBE, the cat spent significantly more time at the end of the box at which Harary was asked to position himself while out of his body (see Fontana 2005). These results support the conclusion not only that Harary was indeed out of his body, but that he could travel to a designated location (his own apartment), position himself in a particular place, and be 'seen' there by his pet cat.

Does a Type 2 OBE, in which the individual visits what is said to be the astral world, provide a more advanced experience than Type 1 in which one remains in the physical world? We don't know. However, there are many accounts, particularly from India, of gurus who visited their disciples while out of their bodies, and were seen by more than one person at the same time. There are also references to the same gurus visiting higher worlds. So the answer is, perhaps, that it depends upon the degree of control that the individual has over the OBE. If their consciousness runs continually throughout dreaming sleep and non-dreaming sleep, it may be that this allows them literally to leave their bodies at will. One of the difficulties in getting to know more about such things is that advanced gurus will rarely talk about their personal experiences. They simply tell us that as one advances in meditation and other spiritual practices, these so-called paranormal abilities (referred to as *siddhis*) usually arise of their own accord. But they also tell us that we should never make them the object of our meditation and other spiritual practices, as to do so distracts us from the real purpose of these practices and risks strengthening the ego and self-pride. This is also the reason why they do not talk of their own experiences, as to do so would encourage others to practise simply in order to have similar experiences themselves.

Leaving the Body During the Night

The mystery traditions teach that the soul body leaves the physical body every night during sleep, and remains located just above it. Usually this happens during dreamless sleep, and the experience is not remembered in the morning. But these traditions also tell us that sometimes the soul body goes on its travels during dreaming sleep, and that we have dim recollections of these travels in the morning. On one occasion I saw a dear friend of mine, Ingrid Slack, while she was out of her body, as clearly and as unmistakably as if she were physically present – so much so that I assumed she was present, and spoke to her in surprise at her unexpected arrival in my house. The experience happened early in the morning as I awoke from sleep, and wide awake I raised myself on my left elbow and turned my whole body to face her as I spoke. However, she seemed not to hear me, and looked steadily ahead of herself with a preoccupied expression. As I waited for her to answer me she gradually became transparent so that I could see the window through her, and suddenly was gone. Speaking to her by telephone on the next day, she told me she remembered waking from what she described as a 'psychic dream' and with the pressing thought in her head that, although she could not remember the exact details of the dream, she must 'Tell David about it'. It seems possible that the 'psychic dream' was in fact her out-of-body experience, which she obviously connected in some way with me (a full account of this experience is given in Fontana 2005).

Why couldn't Ingrid remember the details of her OBE when she awoke? As with dreams, there appears to be some kind of barrier that we cross when we return from an OBE to waking consciousness. The barrier is there for a good reason, as we obviously need to be able to distinguish between OBE and dream memories on the one hand, and waking memories on the other. However, if consciousness could be made to run continuously throughout the hours of sleep we would be able both to remember the former experiences *and* not to confuse them with waking experiences. We are unable to see past the barrier between sleep and waking experiences primarily because we have lost the powers of attention necessary to enable us to know what is going on in our own minds. In earlier centuries our very survival depended upon the ability to pay close attention to each moment of the experiences taking place both in the inner and the outer world. Modern life, which has removed the need for us to find our own food and to keep ourselves safe from the dangers posed by wild animals or equally wild men and women, has in consequence removed the need for us to pay close attention to the outside world. At the same time, our attention to the inner world is continually distracted by the myriad artificial (and typically manic) sights and sounds that the media continually forces upon our field of vision. Little space is left for the steady, quiet, focused attention that allows us to take note of the real nature of what is around us and what is going on inside us.

The main value of an OBE is, as the above quotation from Butler indicates, that it can demonstrate you are not your physical body. This is particularly true for those people who can actually see the physical body while they are separate from it. Rosie, who has had frequent spontaneous OBEs, in her signed statement for me even writes of unsuccessful attempts during a Type 1 OBE to wake up her husband, who she could see asleep next to her physical body, in order to draw attention to her separation from it. The same awareness of physical surroundings is also possible when the OBE is deliberately induced. Clare induced her OBE by a well-tried method that involved lying comfortably on her bed with the elbow of her right arm resting beside her and her forearm raised in the air so that if she dozed it would fall and awaken her, while at the same time becoming particularly aware of the sensation of her body against the bedclothes and then imagining that it was sinking down through the bed. A psychologist with a senior university teaching post and with an extensive knowledge of meditation and other psycho-spiritual practices, Clare, abruptly found herself out of the body and standing beside her bed, fully clothed and aware of the objects around her in the room. Having satisfied herself that consciousness can indeed leave the physical body, she became rather bored and, to her later regret, simply decided to return to it without further exploration simply by thinking herself back into it.

Thinking oneself back into the body is indeed one of the quickest ways of ensuring this return. There are now many books written from first-hand experience that attest to this, and I would particularly recommend two of Robert Monroe's books (Monroe 1972 and 1994). Monroe, whose first experiences were spontaneous, studied all aspects of the out-of-body experience (together with any possible dangers) probably in more detail than any other writer. As someone who does not come from any of the mystery traditions and who was taken by surprise by his experiences, Monroe details all the evidence he gained (such as visiting friends and later confirming with them that he had correctly witnessed their actions) that convinced him he really was out of the physical body.

Spontaneous OBE

Although under certain circumstances OBEs can be induced, they may also occur spontaneously. Sometimes this happens when the individual is faced by a sudden life-threatening event, but at other times it can happen for no known reason. I first heard about OBEs many years ago, just after leaving school, when the brother of a friend of mine woke one night to find himself suspended above his body. In a state of panic he 'forced' himself back into his body so abruptly that the repercussion was like a physical shock and he lay sweating on his bed. Subsequently I have spoken to many people who have experienced spontaneous OBEs, and have had minor experiences of this kind myself.

Often spontaneous OBEs are associated with sleep. The individual wakes to find him or herself out of the body for no apparent reasons. On other occasions they may wake needing to pay a visit to the bathroom, get out of bed, walk to the bedroom door, then look back to see their physical bodies still in bed (one reported method for inducing OBEs is to ensure that one experiences extreme thirst during the night). At other times, the experience happens while fully awake. In one of the cases recounted to me, a young woman, while standing in front of her CD player wondering what music to play, abruptly found herself standing to the right of her physical body watching what she was doing. The reality of the experience was such that she devoted a great deal of time attempting to find an explanation, which was in fact the reason why she consulted me.

Spontaneous OBEs suggest strongly that our consciousness is only a temporary resident in the body. Critics may argue that induced OBEs are simply imaginative experiences brought on by self-suggestion, but this argument does not fit the facts, and is an even worse fit in the case of spontaneous experiences. In many spontaneous cases the individual has never heard of OBEs, has no intention of experiencing an OBE, and is taken by surprise when one actually occurs.

Chapter 7

Visualization and Spiritual Development

The Spiritual and Mystery Traditions

The spiritual and mystery traditions used visualization practices for both spiritual and psychological development. For these traditions, spirituality and psychology have never been seen as separate, but as complementary aspects of the same thing, the unification of the individual self (however this 'self' is defined) with the Divine (however the 'Divine' is defined!). All life – in fact all existence – is seen as emanating from the Divine, from the One, and is therefore part of the whole rather than fragmented into separate, isolated units, just as each limb (and in fact each cell) is part of the body. Furthermore, these traditions all recognize the interdependence of all things. Nothing can exist in isolation. Thus the harm that we do to other beings, to the environment, to the air we breathe, to the ground under our feet and the water we drink, we do to ourselves. Love and compassion, concern and care for those weaker than ourselves, non-violence and gratitude are regarded as central to the right way of being, as are practices designed to refine our own nature, to raise ourselves towards the Divine, and to realize the mystical truth of the essential unity of all that is. And realizing this truth means not simply knowing it with the intellect, but experiencing it at the profound level of mystical reality.

Spiritual Visualization

Visualization lies at the heart of many of the practices that lead to this mystical realization, visualization reinforced by will, by the belief in the possibility of this realization and the determination to achieve it. A good example of these practices, and one that belongs in fact to the Western traditions, is the so-called *Spiritual Exercises* of the Jesuits, an order noted for their scholarship, understanding and commitment to the path to the Divine. Their founder, the 16th-century Spaniard St Ignatius of Loyola, developed these *Exercises* as an integral part of the training of young Jesuit priests, and they are said to bring about profound inner changes. *The Penguin Dictionary of Saints* describes their influence over the past 400 years as 'incalculable, and not confined to Roman Catholics'. In other words, the *Exercises* have been of great value in demonstrating the power of visualization in inspiring and bringing about profound inner changes and in enhancing spiritual development. It is possible that in devising these *Exercises* St Ignatius learnt from Eastern traditions, including those of powerful strands of Moslem mysticism.

The *Exercises* are a good example of one of the major ways in which visualization can be used, although within the Jesuit traditions it is always emphasized that one should only attempt them under the supervision of a spiritual director who has himself had long experience in their use and in their profound impact. For present purposes, the important thing is to recognize the psychological/ spiritual principles that lie behind them, since these are an essential part of all visualizations designed for spiritual development.

The visualizations that make up the *Spiritual Exercises* consist primarily of a sequence of scenes representing particularly significant events of Christ's life, from the Nativity through to the

Crucifixion, the Resurrection, the post-Resurrection appearances on earth, and the Ascension. The details that have to be visualized in each scene are given in the *Exercises*, and the practitioner not only has to create these details clearly in imagination but also 'listen' to what is being said by the people who form a significant part of them. He then has to place himself within the visualization, as if he is physically present, and instruct himself to derive benefit from the experience. The results of each of the *Exercises* are then discussed with the spiritual director, and only when the latter is satisfied that the experiences concerned have been fully absorbed mentally, emotionally and spiritually is he authorized to move on to the next exercise.

Traditionally, four weeks of intensive practice were set aside for the completion of the *Spiritual Exercises*, but this figure related to phases of learning rather than to actual time. If, by his close questioning, the spiritual director judged that the practitioner was demonstrating the effects of the *Exercises* in terms of a recognition of his own shortcomings, of an increase in love and devotion towards Christ and his sacrifice, and of a growing resolve to dedicate himself to the spiritual path, he would be allowed to move forward. If it was clear that he was having difficulties with the visualizations, or encountering inner problems that had yet to be resolved, he would be held back. When necessary, the four weeks could therefore be extended to as long as proved necessary. And even after completing the *Exercises*, the practitioner would return to them frequently, not only to reinforce his earlier experiences but to gain new insights.

For the Jesuit the power of the *Exercises* lies in their ability to open the heart to Christ's love, but even for the layman and the agnostic they demonstrate the undeniable power of visualization practices to effect inner changes. And for everyone they demonstrate the importance of taking time over visualizations and focusing upon each of the details contained within them. Part of the task of the spiritual director (friends can help each other in the same way) is to prompt the practitioner to look more closely when describing his visualizations, and to question him intently on what he is seeing (e.g. 'Is the cave/stable of the Nativity spacious or cramped?', 'Is the roof high or low?', 'How is it furnished?', 'What are the people wearing?'). By having his attention drawn ever more closely to these details, the practitioner is helped to develop his powers of visualization and endue the visualized scene with greater reality – and as the mystery traditions insist when teaching visualization, 'The more real it is to you, the more powerfully it works.' When the moment is right and the practitioner puts himself into the visualization, imaginatively and with great emotion, he actually feels himself fully present.

Another valuable principle demonstrated by the *Exercises* is the importance of including the other senses in a visualization. The practitioner is asked, or asks himself, what those present are saying to each other – and also perhaps what they are feeling. Tactile sensations can also be introduced – the warmth or chill of the stable/cave, the feel of the straw under the feet, the coarseness of clothes against his skin, the smell of the animals present. The combined effect of all the senses adds further to the reality of the visualization, and helps the practioner to re-enter it whenever he chooses, deepening the experience each time. The use of a sequence of interrelated visualizations, rather than restriction to the same one each time, can also prove helpful, particularly if the visualizations are progressive, with each one designed to take the meditator further along the chosen transpersonal path.

These and many other features of the *Exercises* are present in the meditation practices developed in various of the psycho-spiritual and Western mystery traditions. The men and women who developed these practices knew at first hand that they worked, and the fact that they have so triumphantly stood the test of time is a clear indication that they work at a very deep level of the mind. Some may argue that their effect is little more than a form of self-hypnosis, but the answer to this is that self-hypnosis is itself a mysterious process. Attempts to explain one mystery by another mystery are of limited value. In addition, all forms of hypnosis are designed to address particular psychological problems, rather than to serve as a long-standing voyage of self-discovery and self-development.

Before looking more closely at visualization practices we need to recognize that, without exception, all the great traditions stress that we should not undertake these practices with any desire to gain personal power or to strengthen the selfish ego. Such desires militate against success, since one cannot go beyond the selfish individual ego and towards experiences of non-material realities if one's aim is simply to *strengthen* this selfish ego, much of which is in any case only a temporary construction conditioned by our early life experiences. Thus, images associated with this ego (such as those to do with power over others or with self-aggrandizement) should be avoided at all costs.

The Desire for Inner Development

It is unnecessary to spend time pondering exactly why one wishes to pursue inner development. The reasons that come to mind are often no more than rationalizations and justifications, and it is enough simply to recognize that the wish is there. This wishing is part of our inborn nature. With some people it amounts to a fierce longing that can override everything else; with others it is a yearning, as if for something precious once possessed that has since been lost; and with yet others it is a vague stirring of discontent or uneasiness with the way things are, and with the standard answers to the fundamental questions concerning life and death and meaning. Sadly, for so many of us, these longings and yearnings and vague stirrings become overlaid by the concerns of daily life and by the enticements of materialism and of short-term goals and ambitions.

Zen Buddhism teaches that the existential question underlying all other questions is, 'Who am I?' The answer to this question is not our name, our career or even our relationships, all of which are things we have or do, rather than who we are. We are not even our thoughts or our emotions, since thoughts and emotions are temporary things that come and go, nor are we our physical bodies, which are in a perpetual state of change and renewal and will one day die. So who are we? The answer cannot be given in words, since it is an experience and not a set of ideas. And since it is an experience, it follows that it must be discovered for each of us *by* experience. Not experience of the outer world but experience of our inner being. For example, it is impossible to answer the question, 'What is it to be a tree?' since to do so we would first have to become a tree. To answer the question, 'What is it to be who we are?' ('Who am I?') we have to first *become* who we are, which means setting aside self-descriptions and all the myriad things we do with our lives and that are associated with us, and taking the path that leads to what the traditions call our measureless eternal essence.

Internalizing the Divine

Another practice that forms a major part of inner visualization meditations involves focusing solely upon the chosen image or symbol of Divinity, rather than placing this image within imagined historical or mythical scenes, as in the *Spiritual Exercises*. This practice has featured prominently, and virtually without exception, in all the great spiritual traditions as well as in all the mystery and so-called magical ones. In fact it could be described as the secret on which all the traditions base many esoteric or hidden practices. The term *guru yoga* that is given to it in the Eastern traditions explains its nature. The Sanskrit word *guru* means 'teacher', of whom four levels are recognized in the Hindu and Buddhist traditions: firstly, the parents; secondly, school and university teachers and all who concern themselves with our education and our career; thirdly, the spiritual master who leads us on the path of spiritual development and self-realization; and fourthly, the cosmic teacher, the divine incarnation who dwells in the spiritual realms and to whom the earthly guru tries to lead us. The Sanskrit word *yoga* means 'yoke' or 'link'. Put together, the two words *guru yoga* therefore tell us that the practice concerned is aimed at linking us with the Divine or, in the words of some teachings, it enables us to become one with, or to find our true identity within, the Divine; or in the words of yet other traditions it enables us to realize the Divine within us or our own indwelling true nature.

These various forms of words reflect the fact that each tradition has a different concept of the Ultimate Reality or the Divine – call it what one will – for example God the Father or Christ in Christianity, the Cosmic Buddha in Buddhism, Allah in Islam, the various forms of Vishnu or Siva in Hinduism. These different concepts reflect, in turn, the fact that the Divine has to be expressed in a personalized form if we wish to put ineffable spiritual experiences into words. But the important thing for present purposes is that, by quite different routes and at quite different times in history, these many traditions have all developed what is essentially the same type of visualization practice. I give a description of the practice in a moment, but first it is relevant to describe how I know that it works. Personal experience is never scientific in the sense that it cannot be put to the test by others under controlled conditions. Nevertheless, in terms of the deeper levels of the mind, personal experience, assuming it is compatible with the personal experience in these levels reported by others, is the best guide that we have.

Some years ago, when I began to learn Buddhist meditation in the belief (wrongly as it turned out) that the Western traditions had no place for meditation practices, I requested an audience with Lama Damcho Yonten, the Tibetan Spiritual Director of the Lam Rim Buddhist Centre near Raglan in South Wales. He graciously received me in his room, and we talked together for about an hour, though in fact never mentioning meditation on this first meeting. The interview was very helpful in giving me a general introduction to Tibetan Buddhism, but nothing special happened or was expected to happen by way of deep spiritual experiences. However, that evening when I sat in meditation in my own room using my usual practice of closing my eyes and concentrating upon my breathing, I suddenly and totally unexpectedly became aware of a presence seated facing me. You may ask how did I become 'aware' of this presence if I had my eyes closed? The answer is, being of sound mind and not under the influence of drugs of any kind, I nevertheless simply knew someone was there. Although a meditator of several years standing, I had never had such an experience before. Strangely, I had no wish to open my eyes, and even the idea that I might do so never crossed my mind. I was content to sit with this presence, in tranquillity and peace, throughout the half hour or so of my meditation. As the meditation finally drew to a close I equally unexpectedly became aware, without opening my eyes, that the presence opposite me rose into the air until it was positioned over my head, then turned to face the same direction as myself and descended through the crown of my head and came to rest in my heart. There was no accompanying experience of blinding insight, no world-shaking revelation, only a gentle and peaceful awareness of what had happened.

This extraordinary, although somehow perfectly normal, experience remained in my mind the following day. For some reason I felt no surprise at the memory, only a sense of rightness. The experience simply was as it was. However, shortly afterwards I mentioned it to Buddhist friends who were students of Lama Damcho Yonten and who, unlike me, certainly did show surprise. My experience, they informed me, represented a precise guru yoga meditation practised by the lama every day in his room. The sense of presence, the positioning of this presence above my head at the conclusion of the meditation and the descent of this presence into the heart, was exactly the essence of visualization at the centre of guru yoga meditation. Thus, in some way inexplicable by normal means, I had absorbed the lama's practice of guru yoga simply by sitting with him in his room. Let me be clear about this. I had never prior to this experience heard of guru yoga, far less of the practices it involved. The lama never mentioned it to me (no lama would discuss his own practice with someone on their first visit to him). Interpret the experience as you will, there is no shadow of doubt that, intentionally or unintentionally, he transmitted something to me, possibly as a way of introducing me to guru yoga.

I never discussed the experience with the lama, but subsequently, when I joined his meditation class I learned that Tibetan Buddhists carry out the guru yoga practice by visualizing the Buddha sitting before them, with each detail of his robes and even the position of his hands symbolizing the qualities of compassion, wisdom, serenity and final enlightenment that he represents. The lama informed me that a Christian could perform the same practice by visualizing Christ. This teaching provided me with invaluable information for my own practice, and also revealed to me the openness of Tibetan Buddhists (or rather of Tibetan Buddhism as practised by the Tibetans themselves – not all Western Buddhists are equally open) to all spiritual paths ('There are many doors into the monastery,' as another senior Tibetan lama once put it to me). How many Western traditions I wonder would be quite so ready to accept the power and authenticity of spiritual teachings other than their own?

Guru Yoga

Guru yoga involves building up a very detailed visualization of the guru as if he or she is indeed seated directly in front of one. The visualization can be of a chosen representation of the guru taken from a painting or a statue, or it can be built up completely from the imagination. Having built up the visualization, the meditator focuses upon it for the whole of the session, bringing the mind gently and calmly back to it should it try to wander away. As a final stage in the meditation, the image is visualized, as already described, rising into the air, turning to face the same way as the meditator, then descending through the crown of the head and coming to rest in the heart chakra. Repeated each day and over a period of time, the qualities symbolized by the guru then become internalized.

Some Buddhists teach that the guru is the creation of one's own mind rather than a being from outside oneself, and that through the practice one awakens spiritual potentialities already there within oneself. However, in Buddhism there is only the One Mind, of which our own minds are an expression. Thus, to say that the guru is the creation of one's own mind does not mean exactly what it would mean to a Westerner. It does not imply that the meditator, as an individual separate from the rest of creation, is imagining and building up a fantasy. It means that ultimately there is no distinction between the meditator's mind and the One Mind of which the guru is also an expression. The teaching is directed, among other things, towards preventing the strengthening of the meditator's own individual ego with delusions of personal grandeur, as might happen if it is supposed that the guru, as an outside cosmic force, has now invested the individual self with all his spiritual power.

If you have no belief in any cosmic or divine force, irrespective of the tradition with which it is associated, then the meditation is carried out with an image or symbol taken to represent your own Higher Self, that wise aspect of yourself, from within the unconscious, that encompasses your true nature. You can choose which archetypal symbol or geometrical form best exemplifies this Self to you, but it is better to allow it to emerge at some point during the visualization exercises given in due course below. In exercises such as these, some writers and teachers talk of finding this Higher Self in the form of a man or woman, or even an animal who appears as an inner 'guide', a wise person who shows you the way to the knowledge or wisdom you seek, and supports and encourages you on the journey. Sometimes this 'guide' even appears to take on an independent existence. However, it is unwise to attach too much importance to this or to rely upon your 'guide' for advice or assistance on matters relating to the everyday world. Remember that he or she is a symbol of an aspect of yourself, rather than an omniscient being from another dimension.

The Kabbalah

When the Kabbalah, the great mystical system of Hebrew scholarship, was mentioned briefly in Chapter 1, reference was made of the so-called practice of 'rising through the planes' of the Kabbalistic *sephirot* or Tree of Life developed by the Western mystery traditions. Some details of this practice are given in Box 12, and it will be seen that it depends entirely upon visualizing suitable symbols for each of the 'planes'. Chapter 1 explained that the seven lower *sephirot* (in ascending order: the Kingdom, the Foundation, Glory, Victory, Beauty, Power, and Loving Kindness) are levels of attainment or knowledge, while the three higher *sephirot* (Understanding, Wisdom and the Crown) are mystical levels of consciousness leading finally to the Divine. Taken together, and in descending order, these levels are said to be the successive manifestation through which the Divine created the material world. Thus the first manifestation of divine energy in the emptiness that existed before creation was the Crown (the ineffable, mystical undifferentiated Unity of the Divine) followed by Wisdom (the knowledge that enables individual beings and objects to become possible), and Understanding (the ability of the mind to recognize and comprehend individuality) and progressively by the seven lower *sephirot* which are the successive aspects of existence (see Lancaster 2006).

With some exceptions the *sephirot* are usually grouped in

pairs. These are shown below, together with the respective Hebrew term in each case.

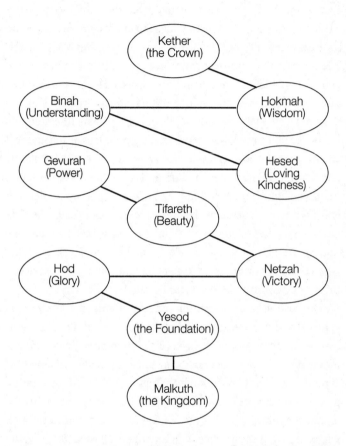

The emanations of the Divine depicted in the Tree of Life apply to all aspects of creation. Therefore the specific relevance of each level of the *sephirot* varies depending upon which aspect we are considering. In the case of humans, the relevance of these levels and the meditative practices associated with them when rising through the planes are as follows. In meditation we have firstly the body (the Kingdom), which we work upon by learning to sit and to control the restless desire to move. This is followed by work on synchronizing the body and mind through control of the breathing (the Foundation), followed in turn by the ability to still the mind (Hod) and then to obtain victory over the thoughts and the emotions (Netzah). This victory leads to entry into the bliss of the spiritual realms (Tifareth) which leads to power over one's real self (Gevurah) and to transcendence over the selfish ego and to the generation of infinite unselfish love (Hesed). Having reached this point, there comes an understanding of true reality (Binah) followed by actual experience of this reality (Hokmah) and finally full realization – expressed in the mystery traditions as the mystical wedding of the material and the spiritual, of earth (Malkuth) and heaven (Kether). Beyond Kether lies Ain Soph, the Absolute, the Divine which is beyond human language and comprehension and from which emanates the Tree of Life. Each level of the Tree has to be worked on in its own right. Success at each level enables the meditator to commence work on the next level, but only when and if this work is done can one enter into and experience this level (see Drury 1979, Regardie 1982).

One of the most reassuring aspects of studying the various spiritual and mystery traditions is the discovery of the important similarities that lie behind the surface differences. These similarities assure us that we are not losing ourselves in the wilderness of superstition and wish-fulfilment. Thus, a study of all meditation practices, whether they involve visualization or not, reveals that the planes identified in the *sephirot* are indeed the planes through which each of these practices will eventually take us. However, the mystery traditions teach that visualization, properly conducted, is a particularly effective way of practising (Box 12).

Higher Self Visualization

A third form of visualization meditation widely used over the centuries, particularly by the mystery traditions, is referred to variously as *The Higher Self Meditation* or the *Inner Guide*

Box 12: Rising Through the Planes

In any practices associated with the Kabbalah it is important to work with a suitably qualified teacher, who can confirm with the meditator that he or she has indeed realized each of the planes represented by the *sephirot*. In authentic Kabbalistic teachings, the meditator is sometimes instructed to visualize a Hebrew letter for each *sephira*, since these letters are said to have symbolic value, and to have been given to humankind by the Divine along with each of the emanations.

In the Western mystery traditions the archetypal symbols of the Tarot cards are more often used for this symbolic purpose. Eliphas Lévi, the 19th-century magus, developed a system using each of the cards from the Tarot major arcana for the various 'paths' between the planes (Lévi 1995), but various other such systems now exist that use the cards to symbolize the planes themselves. Some meditators find it helpful to use a card for each of the individual *sephira* and make their own choice, based upon the symbolic meaning of each card. One suggestion is as follows:

Malkuth – *the Magician* (even sitting in meditation is said to be a magical act)

Yesod – *the Lovers* (symbolizing the union between body and mind)

Hod – *the Hermit* (an archetypal symbol for stillness)

Netzah – *Strength* (always shown in the various Tarot packs as female, and thus as the gentle strength that overcomes the power of thoughts and emotions)

Tifareth – *the Star* (entry into the beauty of the spiritual realms)

Box 12 Cont.

Gevurah – *Justice* ('Gevurah' is often translated as 'Justice', the justice that banishes the small artificial self, the ego, as an impostor)

Hesed – *the Empress* (who symbolizes the creative love that sustains all life)

Binah – *the Hierophant* (the initiating priest, the expounder of all mysteries)

Hokmah – *the High Priestess* (the Mistress of Mysteries, the embodiment of wisdom)

Kether – *the Sun* (the ultimate symbol of divine creative energy)

These are only suggestions. Binah, for example, is seen as female in the Kabbalistic system and Hokmah as male, so you may prefer to reverse these two cards. The fact that the suggested cards are not in the same order as they appear in the pack is not relevant here. They are best kept in the pack order if you are using the Tarot as a progressive path of inner development in its own right, but for all other uses they can be taken in any order, since each card represents an archetypal symbol that possesses a unique value.

The chosen ten cards are visualized, one for each plane, and the meditator then visualizes him or herself entering the archetypal world symbolized by the card in the manner detailed when further reference to the Tarot is made below.

Another method is to use the Higher Self visualizations, detailed in the next section, and request guidance at appropriate points as to the symbols that will take one into each of the planes.

Meditation. Currently it is also extensively used by transpersonal psychologists who find it invaluable in helping clients contact the deeper aspects of themselves. Transpersonal psychotherapists also use a variant called *guided imagery* as an aid in the identification of the underlying causes of psychological problems. Unlike the *Spiritual Exercises* and guru yoga, this form of visualization involves the concepts of movement and travel, and is much freer both in form and intention than either of these two practices.

Read through all the guidelines for this visualization before you try it, and commit them to memory. Your concentration will be disrupted if you have to keep referring back to them. Once the visualization starts, it tends to take on a life of its own, just as in dreams, and it is important to allow this to take its course. Alternatively, you can ask a friend who is also interested in visualization practices to read the guidelines out for you during the visualization. It is better to keep the eyes closed throughout, whether you have committed the details to memory or whether someone is reading them to you. The visualization differs from guided imagery in that it does not tell you what you are seeing or direct you where to go and what to do. Some people complain that when told by the psychotherapist during a guided imagery session that they are 'seeing' a particular object or taking a particular path, their minds keep telling them that in fact they are 'seeing' or 'doing' something quite different. Therefore too much guidance may actually interfere with real self-discovery. In the visualization that follows, you are given the outline, and the creative unconscious does the rest.

As with all visualization practices, it is important to commence by ensuring that you are properly relaxed, and focusing upon the breathing, as detailed in Box 4. One of the best places to start the meditation is with an image that is symbolic of a journey. A stairway leading downwards into the unconscious, or an avenue of trees, or a winding river are all popular examples. Why moving downwards rather than upwards? – because we are moving deeper into ourselves, and the idea of downwards is more appropriate. Some people equate moving downwards as descending to lower regions while upwards represents ascension heavenwards, but we are not talking about down and up in this sense. We need a symbol that opens the way to the unconscious, and for most people the idea of downwards, down from the conscious mind which is usually thought of as being in the head, to the unconscious, which pervades and sustains the whole body, makes most sense.

Choose your pathway and see it clearly in front of you. Build up all the details. You may be about to walk down a stairway, or set off along an avenue between trees, or untie a small boat and use it to take you onto a river, or start out on any journey that makes particular sense to you. Make sure the visualization becomes clear and stabilized before you actually start out. Don't be in a hurry. Take in the scene in front of you. If it is a stairway, what kind of stairway? How wide are the steps? Are they carpeted, made of wood or marble or some other material? If there is a carpet, what colour is it? Are there banister rails, and is the stairway ornate or simple? Make sure the details remain stable rather than fluid and changeable. Make sure also that the scene is bright and sunlit, rather than dark and gloomy. If it is the latter, you have the power to change it. It is your visualization and you are in full control. Now check your feelings. Are you excited or neutral? If you feel any fear, you can stop if you wish. It is entirely up to you what you do. If you don't want to go further, slowly dissolve the visualization, knowing that you can return to it in the future if you choose to do so (but only if *you* choose to do so). In reality there is nothing to be afraid of. You are only going a little way into your own unconscious, which is already there anyway and exerting a major influence upon who you are. But respect your own feelings. In all work of this kind they are the determining factor, and it is not uncommon for people to want to get this far in their visualization many times before they decide to go further. If they decide not to go further this does not reflect badly upon them in any way.

If you are happy to go further and if the visualization is clearly established, you can set off. There is still no hurry. Look carefully at all the details as you pass them. Pause at any point you wish. If you decide to return at any point, go back and retrace your steps until you reach the point of departure, then dissolve the visualization. Assuming that you are staying with it, continue to the bottom of the stairway (or to the end of the avenue of trees or to a place where you can tie up your boat or whatever) and look around you. What do you see? Are you in a room or hall of some kind, or are you out in the open? Remember not to judge what is happening, rating it as either successful or unsuccessful, good or bad. It simply is what it is. And avoid attempting to interpret anything that you regard as symbolic. Like any meditation it is important not to allow thoughts to intrude and distract you. These are activities of the conscious mind, and you are in the process of exploring the creative power of the unconscious.

A Personal Place

The place you are in now is very personal to you. It is somewhere to which you can readily return when you wish, and somewhere that will lead you to other dimensions of the unconscious in future visualizations. For the present, don't try to move on. Sit down and confine yourself to *looking*, in exactly the way in which it has been stressed throughout the book that you should allow yourself to *look* at the objective world. Note colours, shapes and patterns. Note anything unusual or particularly striking. If you are in the open, look up at the sky and register whether it is clear or cloudy. Can you see the sun? Look at the trees, can you tell what type of trees they are? Do they give you clues as to the season of the year? Are they tall and majestic or fresh and young? If you are in a building, look at the walls for pictures or other forms of decoration. Look at the furniture, if any, and note its size and shape. Look for doors leading into other parts of the building – are they open or closed? Look up at the ceiling, is it plain or embellished in some way? Can you see any books or bookshelves? Are there widows and, without moving from where you are, can you see anything through them? Can you hear any sounds? If you travelled here by the river is it still visible and audible?

Add to these suggestions by looking for anything else that occurs to you or that you think important. The purpose of this part of the practice is to help you to start *looking* while visualizing, one of the best ways of improving your practice (incidentally the experience of looking and taking in details during visualizing will help you look more closely while dreaming, and help you spot the anomalies that help turn a dream into a lucid dream). When you are satisfied you have spent enough time on this part of the exercise, remain in the visualization just a little longer. Does anyone make their appearance, perhaps a group of people, perhaps an animal or animals? Do they notice you and speak? If they do, greet them in a friendly way, but don't try to get into conversation. That can come on a later occasion. Don't attempt too much this first time.

When you feel ready, get to your feet, turn around and retrace your steps, or if you came by the river get back into the boat. Don't worry that this time the boat may be going upstream. It knows its own place in the story, and will take you upstream as easily as it took you downstream. Make your way back to your starting point, still without trying to rush things. Take as much time over it as you did on your way down, still noting the details. When you get back to your starting point, turn around and look back at the way you have come, then allow the visualization gradually to become fainter until it finally disappears, and when you are ready, open your eyes.

Why is it important to retrace your journey back to your starting point before dissolving the visualization and returning to the outside world? The reason is that even the first visualization of this kind can take you quite deeply into yourself, and you need to be sure that at the end of it you are fully back in the present. Although visualization meditations are not a form of self-hypnosis, they are in some ways similar. And any good hypnotist will always tell you that it is important to go back, step by step, over the process that took you into hypnosis. He or she will also make sure they remove all the suggestions that they used to take you into trance before they bring you out. Failure to do this can leave some people with feelings of disorientation and heaviness when the session is over, and these feelings can last until one has had a night's sleep and the mind has readjusted itself fully to reality. So to be on the safe side, make sure that you always go back through the stages that took you into the visualization, taking your time over this, and only opening your eyes when you are ready to do so. Most people experience feelings of relaxation and of good spirits when they finish a visualization meditation as they do with all types of meditation, and report that any sleeping problems they may have had disappear or are greatly improved.

Levels of Reality

If the visualization proved particularly vivid, you may wonder what level of 'reality' it represented. The answer is that it touched something of the level of a lucid dream. It created an experience that was independent of the conscious mind, yet that interacted with it. Thus it was a level at which the unconscious and the conscious were knowingly in communication with each other. Normally in waking life we are only aware of the unconscious and its creative power when it allows thoughts and ideas to emerge into consciousness. It is rather like a mysterious friend who sends us things but whom we never see and to whom we can never relate. In your visualization you have been able to see your friend, that is, you have been able to watch the creative process at work as it takes over the visualization from your conscious mind at the start of the journey and begins to create what follows, with all the independence of a dream. It went deeper than daydreams, where the conscious mind remains in control and creates an imagined scenario in accordance with its own wishes. So in answer to the question – 'Was it real?' – we have to say as discussed earlier that it was both real and unreal.

This is of course paradoxical. How can something be real and unreal at the same time? In asking this question we show all the conditioning of our Western education, which is based very much upon an 'either/or' attitude. 'Either' this is true 'or' that is true; they cannot both be true. This is of course a correct approach in many cases, but it must be re-emphasized that in other instances so is the alternative of 'both this and that'. The 'both/and' approach features prominently throughout Buddhism, Hinduism, Jainism and Taoism – in fact throughout all Eastern thought. If a Tibetan Buddhist is asked whether the images one sees in visualization meditations are real or not, he or she will answer they are both real and unreal. This approach prompts us to question what is meant by 'real'. Is the visible world around us really solid or not, 'real' or 'unreal'? In one sense it is indeed solid and perfectly real. We can see it, touch it, hear it etc. Yet in another sense, in the light of the findings from subatomic physics, it is not solid at all but composed of energy which is in violent motion – it is neither solid nor real. The world as we experience it is certainly a paradox, yet both sides of the paradox work perfectly well depending upon the questions we ask. In our daily life the world is solid and real and we could not survive unless we treated it as such; in the quantum physics laboratory it is neither solid nor real and quantum physics could not survive as a study if physicists treated it otherwise.

When we consider such things we can begin to see that it makes sense to speak of visualizations as 'unreal' in the sense that they are not like the seemingly solid world around us, yet they are 'real' in the sense that they have an independent existence within the mind, and it is within the mind that we experience all phenomena. We don't experience the world around us when it is 'out there', we experience it only when our senses of sight and hearing and touch internalize it within our own minds. This does not mean that we should confuse the reality of the visualized world with the reality of the outside world. The two have a different basis of reality, and must be treated in quite different ways, but both in their own sense are real to the mind that is experiencing them. Some of the Western mystery traditions teach that it is possible, through the visualization exercises discussed in the present chapter, to reach a shared inner space – a level of the collective unconscious in fact – where advanced practitioners are able to communicate with and even see each other. Such claims lie beyond the scope of this book (those interested might like to look at Richardson 1985), but it is important to recognize that, in spite of the very many advances made by Western science in all areas of mind/brain research, we still know very little about the workings of the unconscious.

In many ways Buddhism, Hinduism and other Eastern traditions – and to some extent the Western mystery traditions – are more advanced than Western psychology, principally because they have focused for centuries upon detailed first-hand explorations of what happens within the mind. This method, known as introspection, was abandoned by Western science in the 19th century on the basis that we cannot know whether people are really telling the truth about the contents of their own minds. Western science values only public knowledge, knowledge that arises from experimental work that can be observed and agreed upon by all qualified observers, and chooses largely to ignore the private knowledge that comes from observing one's own mind. The problem is that the brain, the visible biological grey matter inside the skull, can be studied by the methods of public knowledge, while the mind, the invisible non-material world of thoughts and imaginings, cannot. The only way in which it can be studied is by turning inwards and seeing what we can find.

Research, which looks at the physical brain from the outside, can certainly see which areas appear to be active when certain kinds of thinking are taking place, and when visualizations are happening and memories are being accessed. But *brain* research is very different from *mind* research since the latter necessitates studying thoughts, visualizations and memories as actual non-physical experiences. Failure to recognize this point is rather like insisting that the electric circuitry of a television set is responsible for the picture on the screen and ignoring the studio that devises and transmits the programme. Both the circuitry and the studio are important and valid in their own right, but they are doing quite different things and must be studied in quite different ways.

The Importance of Repetition

It is a good idea to repeat the Higher Self visualization on one or two occasions spread across a few days, so that it becomes fully stabilized. Don't be tempted to go straight to the place where you ended up last time without going through the process of getting there. If you do, you are likely to find that the visualization is turned into a conscious construction. In other words, your conscious mind takes over (as it so often tries to do in meditation) and attempts to 'think up' the scene in front of you by itself. This prevents the visualization from developing any further, and simply turns it into a series of mental pictures. Instead, as you would if you were visiting somewhere in the physical world, go through the journey necessary in order to get there. Once you have arrived, look to see if anything has changed or if any new features have been added or if (though this is less usual) something has been taken away. Note these changes if any, but do not try to interfere with them.

The next stage in the visualization is to move onward. If you are in a room and there is more than one door, make your choice as to which to use. If you are outdoors, look for another pathway through the trees. If there are no doors and no pathways, ask for them to appear. Don't try to make it happen. Ask and wait, and sure enough a way will open up. Now move forward and take it.

Don't have expectations as to what you are likely to see. Allow it to become clear as you progress. If you are indoors there may be corridors along which you can go; if you are outside there may be divisions in the pathway. In all cases decide for yourself which way you should go. If you are indoors, the corridor you choose may lead you outside, while if you are outside, the pathway may lead to doors that take you to a building of some kind. Keep moving forward until you find a space, whether a room, a woodland clearing or whatever, that has a special appeal to you. This is now what is known as your sacred space, a place within the inner world where you feel safe and at peace. Sit down and take your time here, absorbing all the details as you did when you first entered the inner world.

Edwin Steinbrecher, who has spent many years researching into and teaching what he refers to as the *Inner Guide Meditation* (Steinbrecher 1988) has discovered that at this point a specific sequence of movement – *forward, left then right* – is particularly helpful in leading you to an archetypal figure whom you may wish to regard as your inner guide. There is no need to puzzle over why this sequence proves helpful. Steinbrecher's experiences, both with himself and with his many students over the years, have simply demonstrated that it is. If you wish to try it, get to your feet when you feel ready, move forward, and then turn to your left. Usually a door or a pathway or a tunnel opens before you. Take it and see where it leads, once more absorbing all the details around you. Then pause and mentally ask for someone to appear who will lead you to your guide. The shamanic tradition that once embraced the native American tribes and many of the tribes in Siberia and in Africa, taught how to develop a particular affinity with the natural world, and advised you to request an animal of some kind (a real and not a fantasy animal) who you then ask to turn to the right and take you to the guide. The advantage in asking for an animal is that there is an obvious distinction between this being and the human guide who awaits you, which avoids any risk of confusion. The animal that appears may be a dog or a deer or a wolf or a cat or something else. Its identify is unimportant. Ask it to take you to the right and then walk forward until it brings you to a figure, standing or seated, who appears to be waiting for you. With both men and women this figure is usually male, perhaps because he is not only a guide but a protector, and in the world of archetypes within the collective unconscious the protector is usually a masculine role. Later, even if he leads you to another guide who could be of either sex, he will retain this role.

As with each stage of these inner visualizations, stabilize things by noting all the details of his appearance. If he is robed and hooded ask him to put back the hood, although even when he does the face may not be very clear initially. This is said to be one of the signs of a genuine guide, and the face will become clear in due course. As well as noting his appearance, note what feelings he awakens in you, and what you can tell of his nature. Steinbrecher considers it important to ask him if he is your true guide, i.e. a personalized symbol of your own inner wisdom and if he can protect you in the inner realms. If he says no then he is not your true guide, and Steinbrecher counsels you to look to his right, where you will see your true guide, at which point the false guide will disappear.

Asking for Guidance

What happens next is now very much up to you. You may wish to question the guide, asking him in particular what he would like from you and what he is able to give you. You may wish to ask him to lead you to a place where you can receive energy and healing, or a place where you can find symbols of higher wisdom, or a place where you can find rest and tranquillity, or inspiration for something upon which you are working, or a place where you can obtain guidance on personal problems or clues as to why you have psychological or spiritual difficulties and dilemmas in your life. The only real proviso is that you should ask for a place connected with positive and beneficial issues, both to yourself and to others. Nothing negative or harmful should enter into your thinking or your wishing. The whole purpose of visualization work of this kind is to help you on the path of personal and spiritual development. If you have any other intention, such as gaining advantages over other people in personal or in career matters it is said that it will rebound upon you, and it is unlikely that your guide will stay with you.

Don't ask for too much, either on this first occasion or on any other. These visualization experiences are not going to provide you with earth-shaking revelations. Most of what happens will be in the form of symbols and clues, which your conscious mind has to interpret afterwards. Owing to the dangers of misinterpretation, don't take any big decisions simply on the strength of what you find during this work. However wise your unconscious happens to be it is certainly not omniscient. It can make mistakes, just as can your conscious mind. Gradually, as you gain experience in this work, so you will become better able to decide on what clues to follow and what to put on one side, and on what questions can and what questions cannot be answered. However, never be afraid to ask. Unless you ask, then the inner guide will not volunteer information.

At the close of the visualization, remember to remain with eyes closed when you have come back to the point from which you started, and gently dissolve the visualization. Then when you are ready, open your eyes and be fully back in the present.

Essentially what is happening is that you have accessed that level of the mind from which dreams arise, and moreover have some choice over what takes place, just as you do in lucid dreams. As you become familiar with this level, you can use it for more extensive self-discovery, and are more likely to find that it facilitates the development of lucid dreaming during your sleep. Remember that many of the great traditions of both East and West speak of the necessity of enabling consciousness to run continuously throughout the hours of sleep, and to regard dreams as a dress rehearsal for dying and for entry into the next world. Furthermore, they teach that the immediate levels of the next world are very like the dream world, and that, like the dream world, we can either be carried along wherever these levels take us or we can gain a measure of control over them, as in a lucid dream, and avoid any pitfalls and delusions that may be presented to us.

As you gain familiarity with the inner world, so you will find that it presents you with more and more opportunities for exploration and for learning. The guide will lead you and, provided you made sure on your initial meeting with him that he really is your guide and not a dream-world impostor, will ensure that all goes well. You are likely to find that, in addition to what you learn of your own inner self and the wisdom that it brings, there are various spontaneous changes that take place. Some people report developing psychic abilities such as telepathy, others speak of becoming more aware of the underlying unity of all life, while others emphasize greater tranquillity and a greater sense of compassion, sensitivity and understanding towards all forms of life, whether human or animal or plant. Put another way, they report becoming more whole, more aware of who they are and of the eternal and infinite nature of their own being and of all life.

Archetypal Figures and the Tarot

Within the inner world you may meet many archetypal figures – personalized symbols, as Jung would call them, of the various forms of psychological and spiritual energy with which we are all born, and of which in so many cases we go through life without becoming aware. One way of learning more about these archetypes is through the major arcana of the Tarot cards. The cards of the major arcana, which represent all the most important archetypal images are a great help to the visualizer because they represent images that arose initially in the minds of spiritually advanced individuals in the cultures that gave them birth. (It seems likely that the minor arcana, which also now forms part of the Tarot pack and is the prototype of our modern playing cards, developed independently of the major arcana and had a separate existence until at some point the two packs were put together.) Tarot cards are not a device for telling fortunes, but a serious pictorial guide to the inner world of archetypes, serving as symbols for various aspects of ourselves, some of which we will have already acknowledged but – until we begin visualization and inner work – others of them virtually unknown to us. Because we are all individuals, certain of the Tarot archetypes may resonate more strongly with you than others, and it may be these that make the first appearance in your visualization work, but they are all there to help and to inform you. Some of the pictures on the cards focus upon human characters, such as The Magician, The High Priestess, and The Emperor, while others focus more upon evocative objects such as The Wheel of Fortune, The Moon and The Tower.

As we saw in Chapter 1, the practices developed and used by the Golden Dawn made particular use of the Tarot. Much has been written about the Golden Dawn, both for and against, but its work is worthy of study by all psychologists interested in these inner realms rather than external behaviour. The Golden Dawn Pack and the Rider/Waite Pack are both examples of the cards that the members of the Dawn were required, as part of their training, to design for themselves, following the principles laid down by the teachings of the fraternity. Looking through these or other packs you will find that certain cards seem to make more of an immediate impression upon you than others. This usually indicates that the cards concerned have a special appeal to you, either because they represent desirable qualities you already have or because they represent qualities you hope to achieve. One way of working with the archetypal images portrayed on the cards is to combine them with work on the Tree of Life, as described above. However, when working with them in inner-world visualization it is advisable, initially at least, to choose just one card that particularly appeals to you. Get to know it well. Take in all the details of colour and shape. Note the symbolic objects that surround the central figure.

Put the card in a prominent position somewhere, and look at it frequently. Close your eyes from time to time and try to visualize it. If you find yourself unable to get the picture clear, go back and look at the card and pay particular attention to the details you missed. Supplement this task by describing the card to yourself when it is not in front of you, as if you are trying to describe it to someone who has never seen it.

When you are confident that you can now visualize the card clearly and accurately, and hold the visualization in your mind, you can if you choose use it as your starting point in the visualization practices described in this chapter. Instead of visualizing a staircase or an avenue through the trees or whatever you decided to use, you can start with the picture and, when you feel properly relaxed and ready to begin, imagine yourself stepping forward into the scene in front of you. Don't do so with the intention of seeing the main character or symbol you have just been visualizing. Follow the usual practice of finding the inner guide (if you are quite experienced with the practice by this time he may be waiting for you on each occasion that you step into the visualized world). You may now, if you wish, ask him to take you to the character or the symbol portrayed on the card. Alternatively, you may prefer to choose a different destination, and simply wait for him or her or it to make an appearance when the time is right.

Using the Tattvas

An alternative to using the major arcana as a way into the visualization is to use the *tattvas* (see Chapter 1). Each of the five *tattva* symbols represents one of the elements, earth, air, fire, water, and spirit – choose one of them and set it in front of you as your object of concentration. Look at it steadily until you can see it as clearly when you close your eyes as when your eyes are open. A sense of being at one with the element that the card represents is sometimes reported at this point – for example that you are bathing in water if you have chosen the water symbol (*apas*), that you can feel the healing and invigorating warmth of the sun if you have chosen the symbol for fire (*tejas*) or that you are at one with nature and with the nurturing energy of the planet if you have chosen the earth symbol (*prithivi*). When you are ready, invite the symbol to reveal a landscape, which it will do either by becoming transparent and enabling you to see into the country beyond, or by actually fading into the landscape. Either way you are now free to enter and continue the visualization.

Why should the *tattva* symbols be a doorway into visualizations in this way? We tend to dismiss the 'elements' recognized by the ancient world as an early and not very effective way of trying to identify the individual units that go to make up matter. We now know that there are over 100 elements, ranging from gold to oxygen, each of which is defined as an element by virtue of the fact that it consists of atoms all of which have the same atomic number (number of protons in the nucleus). However, lacking modern scientific tools, the ancients were concerned only with the way in which the world is directly experienced. In these terms, it is clearly made up of solid objects (represented by the element earth), liquid objects (represented by water), gases (air), heat and the forces of combustion (fire) and – in the Eastern system though not in the West, which although well aware of its existence did not class it as an element as it is unseen – the invisible but deeply experienced force known as life or soul that animates the body and departs from it at death (spirit). By the same token the physical body was seen as composed of earth (flesh and bone), water (blood and secretions), air (breath) and fire (bodily warmth) and spirit (the animating force). Our lives, both in our own bodies and in our relationship with the environment, are therefore bounded and defined by the five elements. For the ancients it made sense to believe that we are deeply influenced by the elements, since we are composed of them, relate to them constantly through our senses, and depend upon them for our sustenance and for our very existence. It is difficult to argue with this reasoning and with the way it is backed up by direct experience. We do indeed have a strong affinity with the elements, and if we focus upon our own body while in meditation we can sense our own solidity, the blood coursing through our arteries and our veins, the warmth our body generates, the air that enters our lungs on each in-breath, and the life force, the mysterious essence which animates us, lives in and through our body during our lives, and leaves when we die.

In the light of this, it also makes sense to see our relationship with the elements as part of the collective unconscious and of the archetypal psychological blueprint with which we are born. And as with all the archetypes, representative symbols for each of the elements have arisen from the collective unconscious, and like all such symbols these contain a particular power to engage our attention and to act as keys back into the inner world. The shapes and the colours that make up the *tattvas* are just such symbols. The salient point is that they work.

If you use the *tattvas* as a starting point in your visualization meditation you may find that the landscape that opens to your imagination appears strongly related to the particular *tattva* symbol you have been using. The earth symbol may lead to a particularly lush and pleasant land; the water symbol to a country rich in waterfalls, rivers and lakes; the fire symbol to a rocky mountainous world vibrant with energy; the air symbol to a lofty world of turrets and towers; and the spirit symbol to ineffable symbolic realms of almost pure consciousness. However, one must not undertake work of this kind with fixed expectations. In the majority of cases the landscape may have no direct association with the symbol with which you started. The symbol is merely there to provide access, without determining the scenery to which access is given. Either way, accept what is presented, and proceed as usual to accompany your inner guide. But remember, with this as with all visualization work, you can terminate the experience whenever you wish. Simply express the intention to leave, and you may either find yourself immediately back at your starting point or retracing your steps along the way which you came. Should you ever lose your way, ask to be shown the path you want and it will appear. There is never any reason for fear.

To conclude, this chapter is about self-knowledge. It is for those readers who feel there are inner dimensions to themselves that they have never explored, and for those who feel that these inner dimensions include much of their own spiritual nature. It is for those who are dissatisfied with the materialistic philosophy that argues there is no more to us than our physical bodies, and no more to our lives than the interval between birth and death. It is for those who consider that the answer to the mysteries of existence lies within ourselves, and that the place to look is therefore inside rather than merely outside. It is for those who respond to the old Sufi story of the man who was discovered by his neighbour looking for a lost key out in the street. When asked by the neighbour where the key was lost, his answer was that it was lost somewhere within his house. 'Then why,' asked the neighbour, 'are your looking for it out in the street?' 'Why?' replied the man, 'because there is more light out here.' The story, like many of the enduring stories that are an integral part of the great traditions, tells us in a few words what otherwise we might take many volumes to explain, namely that if you want to find something you must look in the place where it was lost, instead of supposing that you will get better results if you look somewhere else that appears to be easier. It is no good looking for answers that can only be found in the inner world by spending all our time searching in the outer world simply because the outer world seems an easier option.

Box 13: Continuing the Practice

The ability to visualize develops steadily with practice. This book has surveyed some of the ways in which visualization can be used in a number of important areas, but to make full use of visualization it is essential to keep practising – and to keep experimenting. Try out what works best for you. Some people find that a quick glance at something that interests them works as well as looking at it steadily for some minutes. Some people report that certain colours are easier to visualize than others, and that the same applies to certain objects. This suggests the need to spend more time practising with difficult colours and different objects.

Never forget that part of the secret of visualization depends upon really *looking* at things, really *seeing* them instead of taking only a superficial interest in the visual world. Equally, don't forget the importance of archetypal symbols if you wish to explore the inner world. These symbols reconnect us with the collective unconscious, with the psychological foundation of our very being. Carl Jung rightly insisted that we do not know where the mind ends. By this he meant that there may be no limits to the power and extent of the mind when we learn to go deeply into it. The collective unconscious may indeed be an open door that can take us into mental and spiritual realms of which we normally never dream.

And while on the subject of dreaming, remember the importance of making better contact with the magical inner theatre of your dream life. Dreams are another pathway into the collective unconscious, and the more we train ourselves to remember them and study them, the more we can find and explore this pathway.

Finally, remember the long history of visualization. Mankind has always visualized. Had it not done so we would have no great art, no great architecture, and very few of the products of human creative imagination that go to enrich our lives and lift our spirits.

Conclusion

It should come as no surprise to know that visualizing ourselves achieving a goal – providing the goal is a realistic one – can actually help us to attain it. The act of visualizing helps to convey the message to the unconscious that the goal is possible, thus prompting the unconscious to mobilize the abilities necessary for its attainment. We all of us have far more of these potential abilities than we imagine. Our personal unconscious (the level of the unconscious particular to each individual) and the collective unconscious (the deeper levels common to all the human race) represent a veritable treasure trove of dimension after dimension of psychological and spiritual possibilities. The collective unconscious in particular is part of our birthright, but unless we choose to explore these possibilities, then we go through life without even knowing of their existence.

Pictures form part of the language of the personal unconscious and especially of the collective unconscious, hence the reason why visualization practices can often contact these areas of the mind very much better than words. The Western mystery traditions stress that will and imagination represent the essential combination necessary for working with these areas, and that we all possess both will and imagination in abundance if we only care to make proper use of them. Will implies strong motivation together with the confidence that we can achieve, while imagination means the ability to picture the achievement in our mind's eye. Once will and imagination are combined they also open other areas of the inner world that help lead us towards knowledge of our real self and of the spiritual realities that as Professor William James, one of the finest minds in the history of modern Western thought, insisted are separated from us only by the flimsiest of veils (James 1960). Have we the will and the imagination to see through this veil? The answer depends very much upon ourselves.

Finally, since visualization skills are intimately connected with the ability to use not only the so-called third eye of imagination but the two eyes with which we view physical reality, they help us come to appreciate more fully the enchanting beauty of the natural world around us. We come to see it with the wonder and the freshness of the artist and the poet, and to marvel at the extraordinary mystical gift of life itself. Each day becomes a constant renewal of this wonder, and a reminder of the gratitude due for this gift. How strange that we should be given the opportunity to be alive at all!

References

Barlow, W (1979) *The Alexander Principle*, Arrow Books, London (originally published by Victor Gollancz)

Benson, H (1996) *Timeless Healing*, Simon & Schuster, London

Braud, W G (1990) 'Distant mental influence of rate of hemolysis of human red blood cells', *Journal of the American Society for Psychical Research*, 84, 1, 1–24

Braud, W, Schafer, D, and Andrews, S (1990) 'Electrodermal correlates of remote attention: autonomic reaction to an unseen gaze', *Proceeding of the 33rd Annual Convention of the Parapsychological Association*, 14–28

Brook, S (1983) *The Oxford Book of Dreams*, Oxford University Press, Oxford

Butler, W E (1991) *Magic and the Magician*, Aquarian Press, London

Corbishley, T (1973) (trans.) *The Spiritual Exercises of St Ignatius Loyola*, Wheathamstead, Herts., Anthony Clarke

Drury, N (1979) *Inner Visions*, Routledge & Kegan Paul, London and Boston

Edwards, B (1981) *Drawing on the Right Side of the Brain*, Souvenir Press, London

Fontana, D (1990) *Dreamlife,* Element Books, Shaftesbury

— (1993) *The Secret Language of Symbols*, Duncan Baird Publishers, London; and Chronicle, San Francisco

— (1994) *The Secret Language of Dreams*, Duncan Baird Publishers, London; and Chronicle, San Francisco

— (2005) *Is There an Afterlife?* John Hunt, Alresford

Freud, S (1953) *The Interpretation of Dreams*, Vols. IV and V of the Collected Works, Hogarth Press, London (first published 1900)

Gallwey, W T (1975) *The Inner Game of Tennis*, Jonathan Cape, London (reissued by Pan Books 1986)

Goleman, D, and Gurin, J (1993) (eds.) *Mind Body Medicine*, Consumers Union/Fetzer Institute, New York

Hart, G (1986) *Egyptian Gods and Goddesses*, Routledge & Kegan Paul, London

Herrigel, E (1953) *Zen in the Art of Archery*, (trans. by R F C Hull) Routledge & Kegan Paul, London

Horwitz T, Kimmelman, S, and Lui, H H (1982) *Tai Chi Ch'uan: The Technique of Power*, Rider, London

James, W (1960) *The Varieties of Religious Experience*, Fontana Books, London (first published 1903)

Jung, C G (1956) *Symbols of Transformation*, Vol. 5 of the Collected Works, (trans. by R F C Hull) Routledge & Kegan Paul, London

— (1963) *Memories, Dreams, Reflections*, (trans. by R F C Hull) Routledge & Kegan Paul, London

— (1968) *The Archetypes and the Collective Unconscious*, Vol. 9 Part 1 of the Collected Works, (trans. by R F C Hull) Routledge & Kegan Paul, London

— (1971) *Psychological Types*, Vol. 6 of the Collected Works, (trans. by R F C Hull) Routledge & Kegan Paul, London

Kilner, W J (1965) *The Human Aura*, University Books, New York (revised edition)

Koichi, T (1982) *Ki in Daily Life*, Ki No Kenkyukas, Tokyo and Harper & Row, New York

LaBerge, S (1985) *Lucid Dreaming: The Power of Being Awake and Aware in Your Dreams*, Tarcher, New York (re-issued by Ballantine Books)

— (1990) *Exploring the World of Lucid Dreaming*, Ballantine Books, New York

Lancaster, B L (2006) *The Essence of Kabbalah*, Arcturus/Foulsham, London

Lévi, Eliphas (1995) *Transcendental Magic*, Bracken Books/Studio Editions, London (originally published 1855 as two volumes in French, *Dogme de la Haute Magie et Rituel*)

Monroe, R A (1972) *Journeys Out of the Body*, Souvenir Press, London (reissued by Corgi Books)

— (1994) *Ultimate Journey*, Doubleday, New York

Moody, R, and Perry, P (1994) *Reunions: Visionary Encounters with Departed Loved Ones*, Ballantine Books, New York

Moss, T (1979) *The Body Electric*, Tarcher, Los Angeles

Moyers, B (1993) (ed.) *Healing and the Mind*, Doubleday, New York

Muldoon, S, and Carrington, H (1987) *The Phenomena of Astral Projection*, Rider, London (first published 1951)

— (1992) *The Projection of the Astral Body*, Rider, London (first published 1929)

Payne, P (1981) *Martial Arts: The Spiritual Dimension*, Thames & Hudson, London

Radin, D (1997) *The Conscious Universe*, HarperEdge, San Francisco

Regardie, I (1972) *The Tree of Life*, Samuel Weiser, York Beach, Maine USA

Regardie, I (1982) *Foundations of Practical Magic*, Thorsons, Northamptonshire

Richardson, A (1985) *Dancers to the Gods: The Magical Records of Charles Seymour and Christine Hartley 1937–1939*, Aquarian Press, Wellingborough, Northants

Sabom, M B (1998) *Light and Death*, Zondervan, Grand Rapids Michigan

Schmidt, S, Schneider, R, Utts, J, and Wallach, H (2002) 'Remote intention on electrodermal activity: two meta-analysis', *Journal of Parapsychology*, 66, 3, 233–234

Shattock, E H (1979) *Mind Your Body*, Turnstone Press, Wellingborough

— (1982) *A Manuel of Self-Healing*, Turnstone Press, Wellingborough

Simonton, C, Matthews-Simonton, S, and Creighton, J (1978) *Getting Well Again*, Tarcher, Los Angeles

Steinbrecher, E C (1988) *The Inner Guide Meditation*, Samuel Weiser, York Beach, Maine

Tart, C (1989) *Open Mind, Discriminating Mind*, Harper & Row, San Francisco

Wiseman, R, and Schlitz, M (1997) 'Experimenter effects and the remote detection of staring', *Journal of Parapsychology*, 61, 197–208

Index